▪ AFTER ▪

31
1
2
3
4
5

To my family, for all their love and support

All inquiries should be addressed to:
Barron's Educational Series, Inc.
250 Wireless Boulevard
Hauppauge, New York 11788

Library of Congress Catalog Card No. 91-13511

International Standard Book No. 0-8120-4477-0

Library of Congress Cataloging in Publication Data
Paige, Michele Anna.
After the SATs : an insider's guide to freshman year /
Michele Anna Paige.
p.   cm.
Includes index.
ISBN 0-8120-4477-0
1. College student orientation—United States. 2. Study, Method
of. 3. College students—United States—Conduct of life.
I. Title.
LB2343.32.P35   1991
378.1'98—dc20   91-13511
                                                        CIP

PRINTED IN THE UNITED STATES OF AMERICA

1234   5100   987654321

Contents

Introduction

Do you remember your first day, week, or year of high school? Would you do some things differently if you had to do it all over again? I know I would. This book is designed to give you the advantages of hindsight, even though you're just getting started. Why learn from your own mistakes when you can learn from those of others?

Most college students learn the academic ropes as I did—through a process of trial and error. This is a highly ineffective method. You waste a lot of time following dead ends and going in circles. Somewhere near the end of sophomore year, students start to work the college system effectively, but by then it's time to think about graduate exams, employment, and professional and graduate schools.

If you know in advance what to expect, you'll make the adjustment from high school to college easier and faster. When you go to the dentist, don't you feel better if you know what's going to happen ahead of time? With your eyes closed, head back, and mouth open, it's a little disconcerting when a whirring sound and the smell of burning porcelain are the first warnings you get about the drill. Don't get me wrong. College isn't one big prolonged trip to the dentist. Although college life will be difficult at times, you will find it very very exciting. Trust me.

Why should you choose this book? When I went to the bookstore to get information about college life, I realized that most of the books were written by people who graduated from college years ago. As time goes by, the human mind tends to block out the bad times and remember only the good times. So what you get is an idealized portrayal of the college experience. This book, however, is written by me, a student. That's right. I'm in my messy dormitory room (you can always tell the degree of stress I'm experiencing by the messiness of my room), listening to music and writing this on my computer. You won't find any teary eyed nostalgia in this book; I remember the rough times quite well.

Because these authors graduated from college 10 or 20 years ago, much of their information is outdated. One author urged students to make use of their college's typewriter facilities when doing reports. Typewriters? You'll be hard pressed to find even a handful of students with typewriters on a campus today. Colleges now have computer clusters that can be accessed twenty-four hours a day; most students can't imagine life without such facilities.

Furthermore, all the books on the market tell you how to survive college, whereas my book helps you not only survive but *succeed* in college. Why settle for passing grades when you can get all As? This book will show you how to succeed inside and outside the classroom! The vast majority of books on college life deal only with academics. The advice they do provide seems to concentrate on the mundane and is of dubious value. Some authors would have you confer with your professor about what color notebook to buy; others go into excruciating detail about using the library, leading readers to wonder if these authors weren't hassled librarians in previous lives! Those books that attempt to be comprehensive often fall woefully short. One book devotes about one hundred pages to the topic of packing and fewer than thirty-five to academic concerns.

Those students who already know why they want to go to college will benefit most from this book. When you go to the dentist, you know you're there to have your cavity filled so that your tooth won't ache anymore. Knowing what you want makes the experience worthwhile and bearable. The same goes for the college experience. What incentive do you have for staying up late and finishing that report, getting up early for class, missing a party in order to study? Take a second now and think about your reasons for going to college. Do you want to attend college because:

- You want to get a better job upon graduation?
- It's a stepping stone to graduate or professional school?
- You want to avoid getting a job in the real world for a few more years?
- You don't have any skills that people will pay for?
- You want to explore your interests and abilities further?

You may be going to college for a combination of reasons. Knowing what you want will make it easier to prepare for the arduous (but rewarding) tasks ahead. Good luck!

1

Acceptance!
Now What?

Over the summer, you will receive a lot of mail from your college. You will get a packet containing a course announcement booklet, preregistration forms, a roommate selection questionnaire, a room and dorm selection sheet, and a meal contract. Depending on your interests and past history, you will receive mail from the leaders of certain activities and groups, such as the football coach, music director, and debate team. Make sure to fill out the forms and send them in promptly. Chapter 3 will guide you through the preliminary course selection process.

LIVING ARRANGEMENTS

For one reason or another, you may not have any choice in your living arrangements. For instance, you and the majority of your classmates may have to live at home (or at your permanent address) because you attend a commuter college. On the other hand, if you live in New York and go to school in California, you will have to make some type of temporary living arrangements (i.e., on-campus or off-campus college-owned room, suite, or apartment).

If you have a choice, however, I recommend you live on campus, even though, as a home commuter, you will enjoy certain of these advantages:

- You won't have to pay for room and board.
- You won't have any roommate problems. You will enjoy plenty of privacy and all the comforts of home.
- You won't suffer from homesickness.
- Since your home surroundings are very familiar, you won't have to make the physical, emotional, psychological, and mental adjustments that dorm life entails.
- Your grades will probably be better than those of noncommuting freshmen because of the clear separation between your social and academic life.

Commuting from home, however will cost you a great deal in terms of time, energy, and money and will severely hamper your social life. Commuter students, especially those who attend collegiate schools, often feel alienated from their school and peers; family obligations and transportation difficulties hinder them from becoming involved in campus activities. Moreover, if you commute, your social life won't be as full because you won't meet as many of your classmates. Living away from home forces you to learn to make friends, become more "social," and deal with people out of sheer necessity.

The experience of living with your peers in a dormitory, although trying at times, helps you to become more responsible, because you won't have your parents, siblings, or high school chums to depend on anymore. You will decide for yourself whether to go to bed at midnight or five in the morning. If you live at home, your parents may prevent your having any control or responsibility via the "you are living under our roof" threat, so that, aside from some academic aspects, college life may just seem like an extension of your high school days.

If you must commute for part or all of your college career, you should make special efforts to immerse yourself in college life. Stay on campus and frequently use campus facilities (e.g., the gymnasium, cafeteria, and student union lounges) in order to come in contact with as many of your classmates as possible. For instance, instead of studying at home, study in the main library or in the dormitory lounges. If you need employment, look into the possibilities of an on-campus job. Get heavily involved in extracurricular activities so that you can enjoy yourself and at the same time become more responsible and meet new people.

Even if you spend many, many hours of your day on campus, you will still have to deal with your parents every day. Before school starts, you and your parents should reevaluate your relationship. Discuss the type of relationship you would like to have with them. Remember that you won't be able to win any concessions from them if you don't show them that you are responsible.

Freshmen who are going to live on campus may be able to choose from among different types of living arrangements. Do you want an off-campus apartment or an on-campus room? If you choose on-campus accommodations, would you prefer a single, double, or triple room or a suite (i.e., a couple of rooms with a common bathroom and lounge)? Moreover, some students can choose between a coed and a single-sex dormitory or between an integrated (freshman and upperclassmen together) dormitory and an all-freshmen one.

For your first year at college, I recommend you choose an on-campus dormitory close to the center of campus. This is the best arrangement for freshmen because it's cheap, safe, and convenient. If you live off-campus, your apartment may be far from the main campus and you may need to pay for transportation. This may well discourage you from joining many extracurricular activities, isolating you from people your own age. Apartments close to the center of campus are very much in demand and as a result are very expensive. Prices for college-owned accommodations, however, are predictable and consistent. With an apartment, your utility bills may fluctuate from month to month; if your apartment lease runs for a year instead of eight months, you may need to sublease the apartment for the spring break and the summer months. In the end, the extra freedom an off-campus apartment affords might not be worth all the hassle.

Despite the potential for problems and inconvenience, some freshmen insist on taking off-campus apartments. If you do, first check with your school's housing office for a listing of acceptable apartments, although such a listing doesn't guarantee that you'll get cockroach-free accommodations or an honest landlord who will give you enough heat during the winter.

If you do live on-campus, choose a dormitory that houses only freshmen (with the exception of your residential counselors and a few scattered upperclassmen). Although freshmen dormitories are LOUD, you will very quickly meet many students in your own class. This won't be difficult at all since freshmen are very friendly; all you have to do is open your door and students will come by to introduce themselves and talk. Upperclassmen tend not to be as friendly and outgoing as freshmen because they don't have the same need to make new friends.

Most colleges allow students to choose between coed and single-sex dormitories. If privacy is important to you, you may be more comfortable in a single-sex dorm, although, since most colleges don't regulate the comings and goings of visitors, students of the opposite sex will be around more often than not, making the whole idea of a single-sex dormitory more a myth than a reality. You'll probably be just as comfortable in a coed dorm.

If you intend to live in college-owned housing, you may have a choice between a single, double, or triple room or a suite. If possible, get your own room. Many students have problems with their assigned roommate(s) (the chances of harmony decrease as the number of roommates increases). Such friction invariably affects the roommates academically, emotionally, physically, socially, and psychologically. Some people, however, argue that the experience is good practice for cohabitation later. I don't think it prepares students for anything they will encounter later in life; how many people will live with a complete stranger in a room the size of a telephone booth? Some point out that students might want roommates to stave off feelings of loneliness, but the reality is that you will have plenty of people to talk to and visit. With so many people living in such close quarters, you will be hard pressed to have any privacy unless you have your own room.

A suite arrangement gives you the privacy of your own room, yet allows you to socialize in the living room. This living arrangement is best for upperclassmen who can surround themselves with their friends.

ROOMMATES

Some colleges require every freshman to have a roommate. If you are destined to have one, you will receive a questionnaire asking about your living habits and preferences. Since roommates are chosen on the principle of birds of a feather get along better together, be honest with your answers. Otherwise, you will be paired with someone whose lifestyle is the polar opposite of yours. You will be asked to answer questions like:

- Do you smoke? If so, how often? Do you mind if your roommate smokes?
- What type of music do you prefer? Do you listen to music often? Do you study with music?
- Are you neat or sloppy? Do you mind a messy roommate?
- What time do you go to bed?
- What are your hobbies and interests?
- Do you prefer studying or socializing in your room?
- Would you mind living with multiple roommates?

Your roommate will be chosen based on your sex and your answers to the roommate questionnaire. As you've already suspected, this is not a foolproof system; the results are probably no better than those of a random computerized process. Statistics show that more than half of all sophomores no longer talk to their freshmen roommates.

You don't have to leave your roommate selection in the hands of the school computer or dean. If you meet someone you like during the college's open house, you and the other person can write letters to the residential life office requesting each other as roommates.

Many freshmen decide to room with a friend from high school. Is this a good idea? I think so. Not only will you feel better knowing that you made your own choice, but you'll also be able to bypass many of the most common roommate problems and concentrate more fully on getting acclimated to other aspects of college. You may hate each other by the end of the semester. There is always a chance that this might happen, but the odds that you won't get along with your assigned roommate are even greater. If you do have problems with someone you already know, you will probably be more likely to discuss the situation openly than you would if it were someone you don't know.

In all probability you and your best friend will get along so well that you will never leave each other's company. Although this relationship can help you get through the initial stresses of college life, it will hamper your overall social growth. You both need to meet new people and socialize independently of each other.

If you don't know anyone at your school, you'll have no alternative other than letting the computer decide your fate. Once you fill out the roommate preference sheet and receive the name, phone number, and address of your roommate-to-be, call him or her so that you will feel less anxious about meeting in September. When you call:

- Be relaxed and positive.
- Try to decide who will bring what. Don't volunteer to bring all the expensive things to share because you may not like the way your roommate takes care of them.
- Find out the date your roommate plans to arrive on campus. It would be unfortunate if one of you got to the room first and picked the best bed, mattress, and closet.
- Don't read too much into what is said on the phone; both of you will be tense and nervous. Awkward things are bound to be said.

THINGS TO BRING

Unless you are a commuter student living at home, you will have to pack for the move into your dormitory. You should start packing at least three weeks before you intend to leave for school. Most first-year students live in small dormitory rooms that come furnished with all or most of these bare necessities: a desk, a chair, a dresser, a bed with a saggy mattress, a pillow, a wall mirror, shades, a bookcase, and a smoke detector. Check with your school officials for the exact room furnishings they provide. Since your room probably won't have a rug, fridge, loft, floor or desk lamp, or curtains, you might want to bring them. Most of these are necessities, the rest will make your life more pleasant. You don't, however, have

to go overboard like some students and bring sofas, lounge chairs, and bars to make your dormitory room livable and comfortable.

CLOTHES

As you pack your clothes, keep in mind the type of climate that prevails in the college town. Some students wait until they go home over the Thanksgiving recess to get their winter clothes, but this is practical only for those who have access to a car. Since most colleges allow students to keep their personal belongings in their rooms over the January break, you should bring enough clothes in September to last you the whole year.

Since many students hate doing laundry, it's a good idea to bring as many clothes (especially underwear and socks) as you can. Leave a change of clothes behind so that you don't have to pack when you decide to go home. Many students wait until they arrive on campus to buy clothes because they want to check out what their peers will be wearing before investing in their wardrobes.

Most college students dress very casually. If you don't believe me, just look at the students pictured in the college catalogue. If you need new clothes, buy them in your own town. College town stores tend to overprice everything. Furthermore, when you get to college you will be too busy with Orientation Week and the start of classes to spend time shopping—and even if you do shop, you might not even find what you need!

Below is a checklist of those clothes you won't want to forget (some items obviously apply to only one sex):

underwear and socks	sneakers
jeans, slacks or some type of pants	sweaters and sweatshirts
	jacket
shirts (long-and short-sleeved)	overcoat
	hat
shorts	scarf
pajamas or sweats	gloves and mittens
dresses and skirts	raincoat
belts	umbrella
shoes (casual and dress)	rubber boots
slippers	

appropriate sports clothing and gear (i.e., swimming trunks, tennis outfit)

business wear (dress suit and tie and jacket) for job interviews

formal wear and accessories (i.e., evening dress or long skirt and blouse with suitable purse and shoes; tuxedo or dark suit with tie and vest)

APPLIANCES AND ELECTRONIC GOODS

Since you aren't going to boot camp, you will want to bring all the comforts of life. Because appliances are expensive and bulky and your room will be small, you might want to talk about who brings what with your roommate so that you don't duplicate appliances.

Perhaps he or she can bring half of the items on the list below while you bring the other half. Don't bring expensive and highly breakable stereos, televisions, and phones, to share because your roommate won't treat your things as carefully as you will. Furthermore, you shouldn't share such things as typewriters, computers, and word processors. Below is a list of the things to consider bringing; not all are necessary. You can hold off on some of the larger appliances (i.e. refrigerator) until you get settled on campus and see if they are really necessary. Then you can rent them.

iron (you can use your desk as an ironing board)
clock radio
travel alarm (in case of a power failure)
vacuum cleaner (if you bring a rug)
hot pot (to make tea, coffee, and bouillon)
phone answering machine
wall mirror
hair dryer
fan
radio or stereo
computer, word processor, or typewriter, along with a surge stopper
refrigerator
tape recorder
floor, desk, and clip-on lamp
extension cords and plugs (there are never enough outlets)
hot air popcorn popper (for low-calorie snacks)
camera
weight scales
humidifier
small television
flashlight

Although I include a television set, some students find it difficult to concentrate on their studies when there is a television in the room. If you're chained to the TV every weekday because of your favorite soap opera, maybe now is the time to break the habit. You can use the extra free time to study, socialize, or join campus organizations. On the other hand, TV can be a great comfort when you're feeling depressed or lying in bed with the flu. You'll have to decide for yourself.

DESK SUPPLIES

You'll save money if you bring your desk supplies from home; prices at college bookstores are very high. These are some suggested items:

pencils and pens	assignment pad
sharpener	wall calendar
glue	bulletin board
scissors	calculator
erasers	highlighters (yellow is
tacks	easiest on the eyes)
envelopes	message board (to hang on
stationery	your door)
wastebasket	tape (single-sided and
paper clips	double-sided)
stapler and staples	stamps
light bulbs	plenty of good quality
white-out	typing paper
address book (with	
numbers of high school	
friends)	

LAUNDRY ITEMS

Every college student hates laundry. Most dormitories have old coin-operated washing machines and dryers in the basement. In order to find these machines available, however, you might have to get up early or stay up late. Since washing is an ordeal, you should bring extra clothing and bed linen in order to cut down on the frequency of doing laundry.

I suggest you pack a laundry bag instead of a laundry basket because the latter is too bulky. Also, bring a drying rack because your clothes will be damp if you put too much in the dryer.

Believe it or not, this is the first time most students will be doing laundry. Here are some tips:

- Wash the dark clothes separately from the light ones. It's worth the extra quarter or so; colors really do run. Red makes all your clothes turn pink.
- Write your name in indelible ink on the inside of your clothes so that you can identify them easily.
- Don't leave your clothes unattended; you might not find them when you return. Read a book or do your homework in the laundry room while you wait. Keep your eyes open because laundry rooms are also good places to meet people.

BOOKS, REFERENCE MATERIALS, AND PAPERS

Your most important book will be a good hardcover unabridged dictionary with at least 100,000 words. Many such dictionaries are

available at a very reasonable price. The paperback ones aren't good enough because they don't give the subtle differences in meanings. Here are some other things you shouldn't forget:

thesaurus

medical book—What do you do for a bee sting? a rash? Even if you don't have to look up anything specific you'll find it interesting reading.

almanac

world atlas

bible

manual of writing style describing the proper format for footnotes and bibliographic references

foreign-language dictionary

one- or two-volume encyclopedia

a selection of your favorite books to keep you company

your high school papers and records. This includes SAT, Achievement, and Advanced Placement test scores, medical and insurance records, high school transcripts, and some of your old high school research papers for reference.

all catalogs, bulletins, notices, and other correspondence you have received from the college. Keep the college bulletin throughout your college career; in all probability you will have to comply with those graduation requirements that were in force when you began college, no matter how much they change afterwards.

PERSONAL ITEMS

Bring as many incidentals as you can; buying them after you arrive can add up to a tidy sum. Most college-town shops are extremely expensive because they know they have a captive market.

backrest	nail files and clippers
prescription and non-	deodorant
prescription medicines	shaving cream

vitamins
various toiletries
cosmetics
mouthwash
toothpaste, toothbrush
soap
talc
pillows and pillow cases
sheets (2 sets)
sleeping bag
family photos
high school yearbook
posters
backpack
Trivial Pursuit or some
   other board or card game
curtain rods
big bathroom towels
glasses and contact lenses

razors
brush and comb
tableware
corkscrew and can opener
sports equipment
overnight bag
identification
trunk
suitcases and duffle bags
hangers
key ring
first aid kit
sewing kit
basic tool kit
washcloths
bathrobe
thongs
shampoo and conditioner
plastic bucket

TRANSPORTATION

Most college students rely on bicycles to get around campus and the outlying areas because they are cheap and easy to store. Bring an old bike so that you don't worry too much about it being stolen. Alternatively, you can bring your car or use public transportation. A car, however, is hugely expensive, and some schools prohibit underclassmen from parking on campus. Furthermore, your friends will constantly pester you to drive them places or to let them borrow the car. Having a car pays only if you live far from campus.

You might want to use public transportation and the campus shuttle service, but be warned that they are usually unpredictable and unreliable. You can conceivably wait in front of the library on a cold Sunday night for a couple of hours before a bus comes. Most colleges have all the necessities (laundry facilities, libraries, cafeterias and bookstores) right on campus or nearby, so you won't have to rely on public transport that much.

THINGS TO LEAVE HOME

If you plan to live in a dormitory, there will be certain things that your school will prohibit. You will find a list of these items in your housing handbook. For instance, many colleges prohibit the use of hot plates, toaster ovens, and heaters in dorm rooms because they are fire hazards. Dormitories are very congested places; knowing how easy toaster ovens ignite, you probably wouldn't feel safe knowing your next neighbor is using one to cook a greasy hamburger. Furthermore, if school officials find you with these prohibited items, they will confiscate them unconditionally.

Pets that can't stay underwater for more than thirty minutes will also be off limits. If you are found with an animal that is prohibited by school regulations, you will be fined. Although, as a rule, fish are allowed, I don't recommend bringing them because you will have problems caring for them. Who will take care of them when you go home over break? When you do bring them home, will they survive the trip? What will happen to them if there is a power failure? Where can you put them in such a tiny room? You will run into some of the same problems with plants.

You would be wise to leave your valuables and cash at home. Unfortunately, plenty of pilfering takes place in college. Thieves find their job very easy because students leave doors propped open. Many students even leave their dorm doors open while they sleep, take a shower, or talk to friends in another room. One of my friends left his door slightly ajar for a few minutes to brush his teeth in the bathroom; when he returned his radio was gone. Don't take any unnecessary chances. Don't bring the Gucci watch your grandparents gave you for graduation. Have on hand only enough cash for a few incidentals. If you need to bring money in order to start a checking account, put it in the form of travelers checks.

THINGS TO TAKE CARE OF EARLY ON

Three months or more before you plan to leave for college you should:

- Decide what type of transportation (car, plane, or train) you will use to get to school and make the necessary arrangements.
- Know how you intend to ship your belongings.

- Reserve hotel accommodations for your parents. You will have a bed waiting for you at college, but your parents won't. Make reservations way in advance; otherwise, your parents won't find a room.

TIPS ON PACKING

Every fall and spring you will have the problems of packing and unpacking. The golden rule of packing is this: Pack only those things you're sure to need. If you are thinking of packing a microwave oven you intend to use only a few times a month or clothes you hope to fit into *after* you've lost a couple of pounds, think again. Keep in mind that shipping is expensive and car trunks have limited space. Every year my father reminds me of this as he employs creative packing techniques in order to get all my "essentials" in the trunk of the car. Your parents won't be the only ones happy that you followed this rule, especially if your room is located on the fourth floor of a building without elevators. Your room will, in all likelihood, be small; don't clutter it with unnecessary items. Here are some tips you might find helpful as you prepare:

- If you are sending your boxes by mail, have the correct address. Also send the boxes early because mailing rates will be cheaper than if you send it "rush."
- If you are using a U-Haul or a roof rack, pick it up in advance.
- Label every box with your name and address. Also put a piece of paper with this information inside the box, just in case someone opens it.
- Make sure you don't pack away your keys or important documents.
- Use sturdy boxes and seal them well.
- Pack fragile items away from the sides and edges of the boxes.
- Don't pack heavy items like books all in one box, or else they'll be impossible to lift. Try to distribute weight evenly in the box.
- Pack an overnight bag so that you won't have to unpack all your boxes the first night.
- Don't panic if you've forgotten something. Your parents will be able to send it by mail. Otherwise, you can pick it up when you go home for the holidays.

2

Your Arrival

When you first arrive on campus, you'll receive your room and dormitory building keys, identification card, post office box number, and orientation schedule. In your room you'll find a campus map, a student handbook, a course announcement book, a telephone directory, an issue of the college newspaper, a student activities sheet, and a list of emergency numbers. Save these items; they will come in handy later on during the week. Before you start to unpack your gear, make sure nothing is missing or damaged. If something is wrong with your room (e.g., chipping paint, broken screens) or furniture, bring it to the attention of the residential life personnel. Otherwise, you might be fined for the damage when you check out at the end of the year.

If you have a roommate, don't unpack your belongings before he or she arrives. In the interest of fairness, you should decide together which side, bed, and desk will be whose. Flip for the best furniture.

After you and your roommate have settled in, don't expect to have as much privacy as you would at home. Most coed colleges have only one bathroom per unit, because most dormitories were originally single-sex. For convenience's sake, students might decide to make the bathrooms coed. Occasionally this setup makes for embarrassing situations, as you can well imagine. The lounge and the kitchen will also have to be shared.

You may not be able to find much privacy in your own room, either. People often drop by unannounced, and your roommate will undoubtedly invite guests and overnight visitors into your room unexpectedly and hold parties every Friday and Saturday night. Moreover, many times you won't be able to talk on the phone without your roommate overhearing everything. The only solution to the problem of privacy is to know your roommate's schedule and schedule your shower, nap, or phone calls for when he/she will be out.

EXPLORING THE CAMPUS

After you've unpacked, the next thing on your agenda should be to get acquainted with the campus and its surroundings. You'll feel more at home once you know your way around. Although your school will probably have organized tours, they tend to be geared to the prospective applicant and his or her parents, who are more interested in the scenic than the practical aspects of the college. So poke around on your own. You might even want to explore with your roommate; sharing experiences is the first step in establishing a good relationship with your new roomie.

Below is a list of some of the support services you are likely to find at your college. Since students often don't know what services are available to them because they don't know the right questions to ask, I have included a brief description of the types of services and support each office or center provides.

ON-CAMPUS CHECKLIST

Residential Life Office

- Lends room keys to students who lock themselves out
- Assigns students living accommodations for first year students and transfers. Holds a lottery for the selection of upperclassmen's rooms
- Keeps a listing of off-campus housing options
- Takes care of maintenance

Deans' Offices

- Advises student on all types of academic and nonacademic concerns, such as final exam excuses, shortened workloads, incompletes, leaves of absence, crisis management, medical withdrawals, academic standing, academic grievances, graduate and professional school admissions, fellowships, counseling services, and alternative study opportunities. The dean's office is the first place you should go if you have any type of problem or question.

Career Planning Services

- Offers a job recruiting program with information meetings and on-campus interviewing
- Maintains a career library with current information on internships, graduate and professional schools, and term-time, summer, and post-graduation employment
- Conducts workshops on interviewing skills, job hunting techniques, and resume and cover letter writing
- Offers individual counseling, career assessment tests, career forums, mock and video interviews, and computerized job matching services

Health and Psychological Services
(separate offices)

- Has registered nurses and emergency medical technicians on duty twenty-four hours a day, seven days a week, and doctors on call
- Offers information, programs, and counseling on human sexuality, sexually transmitted diseases, eating disorders, alcohol and drug problems, nutrition, and birth control
- Provides specialized care (e.g., dermatology, orthopedics, surgery) for those students who have already seen a general practitioner. Health services also provides in-patient care, tests, medication, and X-rays.
- Offers individual psychological consultations, twenty-four hour crisis hotline, programs, workshops, and conferences on psychological concerns

Chaplain's Office

- Provides students with worship opportunities, Bible studies, classes, holiday observances, individual counseling, retreats, lectures, interfaith workshops, and programs on issues related to religion, cultural differences, race, sexuality, and peer, parental, and marital relationships

Police and Security

- Provides round-the-clock protection. If you are the victim of or witness to a crime, report the incident immediately to police and security.
- Operates shuttle and escort services
- Loans engravers to students for marking portable valuables so that these items can be identified in case of theft

Student Activities Office

- Keeps listings, with brief descriptions, of all student organizations on campus. You can ask to be put on a group's mailing list so that you will be kept informed of the group's activities.

Student Council

- Constitutes student organization. If you want to start a new campus group, you will have to get approval from the student council first.
- Serves as a liaison between the student body and the administration
- Has individual officers do service projects (e.g., provide students with free legal consultations)
- Appoints students to committees (composed of students, faculty, and administration), which make decisions affecting life at the college

Writing Center

- Is staffed by graduate students who will help you plan, organize, and proofread any piece of writing (term paper, reports, and applications of any sort). Make an appointment in advance because the center gets quite busy, especially around midterms and finals.

Public Service Center

- Keeps information about local, national, and international volunteer opportunities
- Assists students in finding and creating new service projects

Resource Center

- Maintains a library with information on alternative learning and leave opportunities (e.g., group independent studies, independent study, and internships)

Women's Center

- Sponsors workshops, newsletters, forums, programs, lectures, and seminars on topics related to women's issues
- Keeps a library of books and other resource materials pertaining to women's concerns (e.g., volunteer opportunities in women's agencies)

Third World Center

- Has a library containing information on Third World issues (e.g., career opportunities)
- Sponsors newsletters, student organizations, forums, awareness events, lectures, and workshops for students

Bookstore

- Stocks textbooks, trade books, school supplies, room furniture, personal items, campus clothing, class rings, posters, cards, and snack food. (Be sure to get to the bookstore early because used and new textbooks often go quickly. Save your receipts in case you drop a class and need to return the books. Don't remove the

price sticker from your textbooks; you won't be able to sell them back without the stickers.)
- Gives students tax exemptions on coursebooks
- Permits students to buy merchandise on credit

Financial Aid and Loan Office

- Helps students find and obtain loans, grants and scholarships
- Floats short term loans in emergency situations
- Allows students to appeal their financial aid decisions

Foreign Student Office

- Counsels students on visa, tax registration, and other immigration matters
- Sponsors events for foreign students

Parking Office

- Allows students to rent on-campus parking spaces. (Some colleges don't rent parking spaces to freshmen because space is limited. Upperclassmen get spots on a first-come-first-served basis.)
- Rents parking spaces on temporary basis

Registrar and Grades Office

- Registers students for their courses. (Save all your registration slips because on occasion the registrar makes mistakes.)
- Keeps records of students' current course registrations, permanent and internal academic files, and declaration of concentration papers. Sends out official transcripts for a nominal fee
- Transfers credits from summer school, advanced placement tests, and study abroad
- Changes grades if appropriate

OFF-CAMPUS TOUR CHECKLIST

copy center	bookstore
post office	parking lots
bank branches and twenty-	parks
four-hour automatic teller	public library
machines	service station
grocery store	church or synagogue
restaurants	clothing store
ice cream parlors	art museum
drugstore	theater

YOUR RESIDENTIAL COUNSELOR

Residential counselors (dorm advisor or some similar name) are upperclassmen who have been specially trained to help freshmen adjust to their new surroundings. Your residential counselor(s) will live on the same floor as you and be in charge of a unit of approximately twenty to twenty-five students. You will certainly meet your dorm counselor on the first day of your arrival. Make friends with these upperclassmen; under their guidance, you will learn much in a very short time. If you have any questions about school, ask your counselor, who will gladly help you or direct you to somebody who can. Besides answering questions, a counselor's duties include organizing unit activities, discussions, and meetings; serving as liaison between students, deans, and university officials; mediating roommate disputes; explaining the college's rules; and advising students on the social and academic aspects of college life. For example, on the first day of orientation your residential counselors will organize a meeting and play name games so that everybody gets to know one another. You'll find your residential counselors to be a great asset in your first year at college.

ORIENTATION

Orientation usually lasts anywhere from a few days to a week and helps facilitate a quick and painless transition from high school to college. You will receive a schedule of orientation events when you arrive, and the residential counselors will probably accompany you and your dormmates to each event. Although orientation will seem like a week at summer camp with its many picnics, barbecues, group dinners, all-you-can eat sundaes, movies, semi-formal dances, dorm olympics, games, discussion groups, and other types of get-togethers, it actually serves as catalyst for meeting many new people quickly. Even though you (and everybody) will be self-conscious, don't let that stop you from smiling and introducing yourself. Try to remember each person's name by associating it with the name of a well-known person or the object the name represents. For instance, if you meet someone named Franklin, visualize Benjamin Franklin standing there. If the person has a name such as Paige or Brooke or Holly, imagine a page, a brook, or a piece of holly. The more outlandish and unexpected the association, the better the chances you'll remember it in the future.

The beginning of the semester is a good time for you to slightly alter your personality, attitude, or nickname. Since this is the first time you've ever met these people, you won't feel so self-conscious about your new traits or identity. For instance, if you hate your high school nickname, use a different one when you introduce yourself. After a while it will become part of the new you.

Unfortunately, some students deliberately arrive on campus after orientation because they feel it's a waste of time. These students arrive right before the start of classes and feel like outsiders when they find that all their dormmates have already formed friendships.

EXTRACURRICULAR ACTIVITIES

Extracurricular activities are very popular among college students, and you should make every effort to get into one as soon as possible. By becoming involved with campus activities, you will enrich your college experience. Some of your best college memories will be of the time you singlehandedly fielded a goal in the last quarter or achieved other memorable feats. Moreover, your involvement in clubs and teams will allow you to: 1) meet your classmates and professors in an informal setting to share information and socialize, 2) learn new skills, and 3) participate in college-subsidized activities that would otherwise be very costly. Your extracurricular involvement might even spark new career ideas.

Once you join an activity and make new friends who share similar interests, you won't feel so homesick. Therefore, you should explore your school's extracurricular offerings as soon as possible. During orientation week, there will be an activities fair at which each organization sets up a booth in the gymnasium and tries to recruit members. Since not all of the established groups advertise or have representatives at the fair, you may wish to consult a complete listing of campus groups at the College Activities Office or the Student Union.

Organizations available at your school may include:

- Academic: Pre-medical Society, Model United Nations, Debate Team, National Association of Engineers
- Volunteer: Freshman Orientation Committee, Homeless Action Campaign, Community Service House
- Sports: Ski Club, Ultimate Frisbee Club, Table Tennis Club, Flying Association
- Entertainment/Theater: Ballroom Dance, Piano Society, Production Workshop
- Political: Peace Walk, Young Communist League, College Democrats, Amnesty International
- Student Government: Student Union (S.U.), Finance Board
- Religious: Campus Crusade for Christ, Bible Studies
- Social: Special Events Committee, Film Society, Cultural Activities Board
- Journalistic/Media: Video Yearbook, Radio Club, Journal of Women's Studies, Photo Club
- Ethnic/Racial/Civil Liberties Awareness: Latin-American Friendship Society, African Alliance, Federation of Filipino Students

After you look through the list of activities, jot down four or five organizations that interest you. Contact the leaders of each and find out when and where the members meet. Once you meet the members and find out what the group has accomplished and what its objectives for the future are, you will be in a good position to decide whether or not to join.

If your school doesn't offer an activity that is of particular interest to you, consider starting it yourself. Draw up a plan outlining your new club's objectives and get a dozen or so supporting signatures. In order to obtain student support, you may need to put up posters around the campus. If your plan is approved, you will receive school funding for your group.

Although it might be tempting to join many groups, commit yourself to only one or two; teams and other groups tend to be very time-consuming. You won't be able to dedicate yourself to more than one activity and still maintain good grades. For example, if you are on the varsity lacrosse team, you may practice for about three hours each day and have to attend weekend games. With this type of schedule, you will be hard pressed to find enough time and energy even for your studies. Keep in mind that outside activities are not more important than classes and grades.

Whatever club you join, try to work hard and attain a leadership position. For instance, if you are a staff reporter on your school's daily newspaper, and hope to make it to senior editor, you will have to spend enormous amounts of time writing and researching articles and be willing to help out on a very regular basis. Some truly committed students even sleep overnight in the newsroom because there just isn't any time to return home. Most students who hold high positions in campus organizations consider the effort they put into attaining their positions entirely worthwhile. A responsible position in a group not only looks good on your resume and graduate school applications but also teaches you: 1) leadership qualities, 2) the meaning of dedication, and 3) how to work under pressure. It is more important to be the leader in one activity than a member of many.

GETTING ALONG WITH YOUR ROOMMATE

Living with a stranger in a small room will probably be a new experience for you, since most students have their own rooms at home. Here are some pointers on how to handle the situation:

- Don't expect to become best friends with your roommate. It would be great if it were to happen, but don't jump to the conclusion that something is wrong with you if you don't get along. You don't have to become best friends in order to live in harmony together.

▪ Take special pains to make a good impression when you first meet; first impressions often set the mood for subsequent encounters. Think and act positive; smile, greet your roommate enthusiastically, and think, "We will get along happily and share some wonderful times together." If you show your roommate that you like him or her, chances are your roommate will like you too.

▪ Don't prejudge or stereotype your roommate. Don't categorize anybody by sex, religion, nationality, race, geographic origin, or major. For instance, all New Englanders aren't preppies, all Southerners aren't slow-moving, and all big-city residents aren't callous. Stay open-minded.

▪ Spend time getting to know each other. Sharing thoughts and experiences will help strengthen your relationship. Invite your roommate to explore the campus, shop, eat out, or play racqetball. Give yourself time to know your roommate; some of the best relationships take many months, even years, to develop.

▪ As soon as possible (within the first few days of arrival), discuss each other's feelings concerning:

  ▪ Study habits. Do you both prefer studying in your room? If so, do either of you study with music in the background?
  ▪ Guests, parties, and overnight visitors. You might want to decide on a curfew for visitors and parties. How do you both feel about overnight guests? Some students think it is all right to kick their roommates out of the room so their boyfriend or girlfriend can sleep over.
  ▪ Stereos, noise, and television. What type of music and television shows do you like? hate? When is the stereo too loud?
  ▪ Phone calls and bills. Who will be responsible for the phone bills? Will phone calls disturb you after a certain hour?
  ▪ Bedtime. Are you a night owl? Is your roommate? If you go to bed early and your roommate studies in the room late, will a single lamp light bother you?
  ▪ Housekeeping. Do either of you mind if the common room is kept a bit untidy? messy? really dirty? If you have a semi-private bathroom and kitchen, how will chores be divided?
  ▪ Room decorations. Do the room colors clash? You might want

to coordinate curtains and bedspreads and set up the room together. (Students often hang their favorite posters above their
beds. The problem with this arrangement is that you are left
staring at your roommate's Grateful Dead poster and he wakes
up every morning to a blow-up of Michael Jackson. You might
want to hang your posters on your roommate's side of the room,
and vice versa.)

- Furniture arrangements. Make sure the furniture isn't ar-
ranged so that the room is divided unequally.
- Borrowing and loaning. Can your roommate use your computer
when you are out? Can you use his TV?
- Household expenses. If you share a kitchen and a bathroom,
how will you divide the responsibility for getting and paying
for cleaning supplies?
- Smoking and drinking. Does other people's smoke bother you?
May others drink and smoke in your room?
- Room temperature. If you and your roommate are accustomed
to different room temperatures, can you agree on a compromise?

- Be responsible, considerate, and respectful of each other. Don't
forget to lock the door when you leave (even for a second), or
take phone messages (name of caller, time of call, and caller's
message), or leave the room when your roommate needs to talk
on the phone privately, or ask permission before you borrow
something.
- Communicate openly and honestly. If you have a problem with
something your roommate does or doesn't do, tactfully broach the
subject. Cite only the most important of your complaints. Sup-
posing your roommate blasts music every afternoon and that,
instead of discussing your feelings about the noise, you blast your
radio in return. Try turning down your music and asking your
roommate to do the same. Otherwise, a minor problem can escalate. You must be strong and stand up for yourself. Some students remain quiet and never voice an objection when their
roommate acts inconsiderately until finally, unable to take it anymore, they blow up. The roommate, however, doesn't understand
the outburst because there wasn't any warning that something
was amiss. Both parties become upset, and animosity grows.

- Know when to complain. Don't complain about your roommate because he:

  - Seems depressed
  - Plays only the type of music you hate
  - Keeps his side of the room sloppy

- You can justifiably complain when your roommate:

  - Leaves your room door open when she leaves
  - Smokes, although she wrote on her roommate questionnaire that she doesn't

- Invites his girlfriend to spend the night with him in your room
- Has parties in the room on weekdays
- Does drugs and gets drunk in your room
- Uses your things when you're not around and without your permission

Even after following the above guidelines, roommate problems occasionally escalate to the point where you become homesick, neglect your studies, and avoid your room. Some roommates go to the extreme of putting tape, a sheet, or a wooden partition down the middle of the room. If you can't seem to sort out your difficulties between yourselves, consider asking your residential counselor or dean to mediate your dispute. With another person present, you might be able to come to an equitable agreement. If, however, you still can't work out your problem, you and your roommate might want to ask your residential counselor to arbitrate, in which case you both agree to abide by his decision.

Sometimes roommate problems become ugly. The only solution in such cases is for one person to leave. This step should be considered only as a last resort after compromise, mediation, and arbitration have all failed. Changing rooms entails all types of additional problems. Does the housing office have a room available? If not, is there a waiting list? Who will move—you or your roommate? Who will be your new roommate, and will you be more compatible with him? Often the housing office will delay processing your room change request in the hope that you will come to a reconciliation. If you have a friend who is also having roommate problems, you might request a switch.

In spite of and maybe because of all your roommate problems, you may find living with another student who has a different value system and lifestyle a maturing experience, one that will help you learn and reinforce traits such as sensitivity, unselfishness, adaptability, and concern for others.

HOMESICKNESS

Orientation events are supposed to keep freshmen so busy that they don't have time to feel homesick. Once all the excitement dies out and classes begin, however, everyone becomes mildly homesick, even those students who seem happy to finally be away from the watchful eyes of their parents. Students experience homesickness in varying degrees; your roommate may seem to be affected only now and then, whereas you can hardly get through a day without feeling its impact. (Homesickness is one of the main reasons students transfer and drop out of a college.) Those students whose close high school friends attend the same college won't suffer long from homesickness. On the other hand, the student who has never been away from home for an extended period of time and who has a good home life will be hardest hit.

Sometimes students inadvertently do things that help prolong their feelings of homesickness. For example, some students insist on having their parents stay with them once orientation begins. After you've unloaded your belongings, your parents should be thinking about heading home. Orientation week should be used to get better acquainted with your roommate, hallmates, and school. By having your parents stay longer than a day or so, you risk isolating yourself from your peers, which will only compound your feelings of loneliness and homesickness when your parents do finally leave.

Frequent visits or calls home provide only temporary relief from homesickness; when you return to school Sunday night or put down the phone, your homesickness will return with even greater force. Furthermore, trips and calls home can be costly, in terms of both money and time. This extra financial and time pressure can perpetuate your feelings of homesickness.

Having a negative mental outlook on college life will further aggravate your feelings of homesickness. Some students begin school with feelings of academic and social inferiority; they fear college work will be too difficult and that all their peers will reject them socially. Still others have just the opposite problem; they consider themselves superior to their classmates. Such students imagine themselves much too mature to get involved with the people around them and often stay aloof from everyone. Some often talk on and on about their glorious high school days or put down everybody and everything associated with college.

The cure for homesickness is simple: Keep busy and make a couple of friends. If you are receptive, your unitmates will be your instant family, to whom you can talk whenever you get homesick. Moreover, you should try to introduce yourself to someone new each day. This won't be as hard as you think, because freshmen are extremely friendly. You might also want to participate in extracurricular activities in order to both meet new friends and keep busy. (Meeting and making friends is further discussed in Chapter 10.)

Note: What often begins as a simple case of homesickness quickly transforms into a textbook case of transferitis, the desperate desire to transfer to a new school. Transferitis will be further discussed in Chapter 14.

DEALING WITH YOUR PARENTS

For many students entering college is not only their first time away from home but also their first time apart from their parents. Whether you realize it or not, your relationship with your parents will gradually begin to change the moment you start orientation. Although a few of your friends will seem ecstatic about their new-found freedom, many students will feel a bit intimidated by all the responsibility that accompanies it. You might even try to resist your new status by calling your parents each day and returning home almost every weekend to bother them with every little problem you encounter. Your parents may try to encourage your continued adolescent behavior, especially if you are the youngest child; they won't easily relinquish the control they have over you. Many mothers and fathers don't want to reconcile themselves to the fact that their child is growing up and leaving them.

When your parents return home after dropping you off at school, there won't be any orientation program to help them cope with your absence. Thus, it will be necessary for you to help make their adjustment quicker and easier (which will in turn make yours quicker and easier). For instance, you can help by reassuring them that they still play an important and necessary role in your life.

You want them to know that you still value their opinions and feelings. Although you should seek the advice of your parents, you shouldn't let them make decisions for you.

If you do have difficulties, your parents' first response may be to take care of everything. Don't allow this to happen. You must become responsible and start doing things for yourself. As soon as you show them and yourself that you can act in a responsible manner, they won't feel obligated to interfere, and you won't want or need them to.

By allowing your parents to indirectly share in your college experience, you will further help them adjust. Through letters, phone calls, and occasional visits home, you will be able to let them know how you're doing. Otherwise, they'll miss you and worry needlessly. Call or write your family about once a week. Your parents will be so happy to hear or see you that they'll treat you like a celebrity. Send them pictures of you with your friends and clippings of newsworthy campus events from your school's daily paper or periodicals. In addition, you can invite them and your siblings to visit you during Parent's Weekend. This invitation will please them because it will enable them to better understand college life in the 1990s. If they do come, try to make their stay as pleasant as possible. Before they arrive, clean your room, reserve a hotel room for them, investigate the types of college-sponsored activities that are scheduled, and study in advance so that you will have time to spend worry-free. When they arrive, show them around campus and proudly introduce them to your friends. If your parents wish, they can even attend a couple of your more interesting classes. Be sure, however, to ask the appropriate professors for permission first.

While your parents are visiting, try not to upset them unnecessarily. Parent's Weekend is not the time to tell your conservative parents that there is no God, the bathrooms are coed, and you and your girlfriend believe in casual sex. Save this type of news for a letter.

By being patient and understanding with your parents as they adjust, you will foster a good solid relationship with them. Although a good relationship requires much work, it will most definitely be worth it.

3

Courses

In high school you had little or no choice in what courses or teachers you got each semester. At the beginning of each semester, I always had my fingers crossed for fear I'd get the one teacher that would make my life miserable. You'll be happy to know that you'll be able to choose your own courses in college. Although your school will require certain courses, the bulk of your program will be comprised of classes that you want. Guidance counselors will not periodically call you into their offices to go over your college schedule; academic counselors will not actively pursue you—instead, you will have to find them. Selecting the "right" academic schedule takes hard work and careful planning and is a crucial factor in determining your success in the upcoming semester. Pick your courses carefully!

Since creating your own academic program is a new experience for many, it is important to learn some general guidelines. First, you should read the beginning pages of your course announcement catalog. They describe your school's policies concerning graduation, honors, finals, adding/dropping courses, grading, and awarding of degrees. Many of your questions will be answered in these first few pages. As you skim through the rest of the catalog, highlight those classes that you think would be interesting.

Knowing your college's graduation requirements is imperative. Most college curricula demand that students complete a certain number of credit hours. To determine the average workload per semester, divide the required number of credits for graduation by eight (assuming your school is on a traditional semester calendar). As a college freshman, you will want to take the normal number of courses to avoid overloading yourself. Each class carries a certain number of credits in accordance with the number of class or lab hours that it entails.

Some colleges do not use the credit system but require a certain number of courses for graduation (usually, thirty-two courses). Although each course requires a different number of hours per week, they are all counted equally. Such a system is inequitable, because some classes are longer and/or require science or language labs, sections, and/or field trips. Regardless of the actual number of hours the class involves, the student receives the same amount of credit for graduation. Keep this in mind when you are choosing your courses. You might find yourself on academic probation because extensive laboratory commitments proved to be overwhelming.

PREREGISTRATION AND REGISTRATION

During the summer after your high school graduation, you will be required to preregister for your first-semester courses. Most local and commuter colleges require you to preregister in person; all others send you their course catalog and preregistration material through the mail. Complete your preregistration material as soon as possible. If your course selections are late, you will probably have a difficult time getting into some classes.

Upperclassmen have an advantage in the preregistration process because they hand in their course selection cards during the spring. As a result, by September many of the limited enrollment classes have been filled. To compensate for this, most colleges reserve a certain number of seats in some limited enrollment classes for freshmen. One strategy you can use to ensure a place in a course is to preregister for only limited enrollment classes. This way, you will get at least one of the classes that you wanted.

There is no need to preregister for large-enrollment and introductory courses. Professors admit everybody to these classes as long as they show up for the first lecture. Preregistration for big survey courses is mainly a way to help the college registrar get a rough estimate of the number of students who will be in each class. Based on these figures, the college can make tentative decisions concerning the number of seats, teaching assistants, sections, and laboratory rooms needed.

Preregistration is not a binding agreement. The probability is high that your schedule will change after you have talked with faculty advisors, peer counselors, and friends. This is perfectly acceptable because you, as a freshman, have no previous experience on which to base your decisions. You must, however, know your strengths and weaknesses. For example, if you know that you are not very good at writing papers, do not take more than one writing class, no matter how interesting the other writing courses might seem.

ADVISORS

As a freshman, you will be assigned a faculty advisor or dean and probably a student advisor. Each will give you a different perspective on the college curriculum. Most faculty advisors will only be able to give insightful evaluations on those of courses within their own departments. Peer advisors, however, will only be able to comment on a wider array of courses. Most schools require first-year students to have their faculty advisor's approval before they can register for a course. If you have a question about a course or a department, find a faculty member in that department to help you. Most professors are very willing to talk about their little corner of academia.

Even though advisors' comments can prove helpful, they should never be followed exclusively. If you constantly hear contradictory information or if you have a strong feeling about a course or professor, follow your own instincts. You will learn to use your advisor's comments as a basis for evaluating other information.

ADVANCED PLACEMENT CREDIT
AND PLACEMENT TESTS

If you took advanced placement (AP) classes in high school and did reasonably well on the advanced placement tests, you may be eligible for college credit. AP credit enables some students to graduate a semester or two earlier. Credit can be earned for biology, chemistry, physics, music, English, history, math, and foreign language. You should ask your advisor about getting credit because each college has different requirements. Remember to have your scores forwarded to your college; the scores do not automatically follow you.

Some students think it is wise to retake those classes for which they have AP credit in the hope that they will be easy As. If you do retake the class, the excitement associated with learning new and interesting ideas will be lacking, and you will probably be so bored and uninterested in the material that your grades will suffer. In addition, some of these classes, such as chemistry, biology, and physics, will be weeder classes full of cutthroat pre-meds. Rather than stagnate intellectually, it is best to get credit for your high school work and go on to more academically intriguing endeavors.

If your college does not accept AP credit, some departments (i.e., foreign languages) may allow or even require you to take a placement test. You will be assigned a class according to your score. In many colleges, these exams are rigorously employed to place students; other schools administer them as rough guidelines to be used as the student sees fit. Placement tests are optional in a few schools. Whether the tests are optional or mandatory, you have nothing to lose by taking them because the scores do not go on your transcript.

Most colleges realize that tests give only a rough idea of your ability. The majority of students do not brush up for these exams; as a result, the scores are not as reliable as one would hope. Only you know if the placement tests have accurately measured your knowledge of a particular subject. If your school requires you to take these exams and uses them as strict and hard guidelines for placement purposes, it might be helpful to review the material during the summer. The extra studying might save you from being placed in a remedial class.

A few schools administer mandatory competency tests in English, mathematics, and/or foreign language. If you do not score above a cerain cutoff, you will be required to attend summer school before you enter college. These tests are usually used to spot those students who are in need of remedial help. Aside from reviewing some very basic material, it is extremely difficult to study for this type of exam because it has such broad scope.

CORE CURRICULUM

A core curriculum is a required group of courses. Nearly every college has a core curriculum of some sort, usually consisting of a semester or two of English, science, history, foreign language, and physical education. Many colleges use the core curriculum to ensure that students graduate with a broad-based liberal arts education.

Freshmen are usually advised to get their core requirements out of the way as quickly as possible. This is a good suggestion, but if you have a strong aversion to a particular subject, take the class the following semester after you have mastered the academic ropes.

Most core classes are introductory courses designed to accommodate freshmen. Therefore, core curriculum courses do not get closed out, but inevitably certain sections will be more desirable than others. Word about these sections will spread, and they will close rapidly. Ideas on how to choose and get into a suitable section are found later in this chapter.

SHOPPING FOR CLASSES

Almost every school has a shopping period. If your school does not have a shop-around option, it's a good idea to sit in on the classes a semester or two beforehand. The problem with this is that, as a first-semester freshman, you were not attending college last semester. As an alternative, you can ask your advisor if you can sign up for extra courses and drop those you dislike.

Too many students do not take advantage of the shopping period. These students pick out their classes and just stick with them. If the classes do not work out, their only choice, aside from academic probation, is to suffer through the courses for an entire semester.

It is always a wise investment of time to go to as many classes as possible during the first week of the term. Maybe you will sit in on a class that you cannot take during the current semester but will enroll in later on.

Contrary to popular belief, you can and should shop for your discussion and laboratory sections. An English class, for example, may have several different sections, each led by a different teaching assistant using his or her own syllabus. It is in your best interest to go to at least two of these sections to give yourself an opportunity to choose. Every teaching assistant (T.A.) has an individual style of conducting class. Some T.A.s are more lenient in terms of deadlines and grades than others. (Since most professors curve each sections' grades on the same scale, those students who were unfortunate enough to get the most demanding T.A. will be assured fair grades.)

I faced a section selection dilemma during my junior year. I was taking a quasibusiness course which required a discussion section in addition to lectures. I attended two sections to see which I preferred. The first section had about twenty students and was taught by two very relaxed undergraduates. The second section, consisting of six pupils, was led by a quiet junior. In every section, students were to discuss the assigned business case and hand in a two-page paper outlining the advantages and disadvantages of each discussed strategy. I ultimately chose the first section because the two-member team was more insightful and elicited more class participation. Furthermore, there were no deadlines for the papers. Not only did the other T.A. have a strict deadline for each paper but the case analysis assignments were to be submitted before we discussed them in section.

When shopping around, it is important to go to the very first lecture because that is when the professor explains the content, structure, and requirements of the course. During the first class most professors give out a comprehensive syllabus, which should answer the following questions (if it does not, make sure to ask the professor):

- What goals or expectations does the professor have for the course?
- What will the course emphasize, i.e., will your French class concentrate on literature or conversational skills?
- Does the professor have office hours? If so, what are they?
- Does the class entail labs, sections, or field trips?
- Does the professor take attendance? If so, what constitutes "excessive" absences?
- Is attendance mandatory for sections and field trips?
- How many exams, papers, projects, problem sets, and so on, are due and when?
- Does the professor grade on a curve? If not, what are the usual cutoffs for As, Bs, Cs, Ds, and Fs?
- What percentage of your overall grade is based on labs? attendance? class participation? exams? papers and homework?
- Are the professor's exams multiple-choice, essay, short-answer, or a combination of these?
- Will the material covered on the exams be cumulative?
- Will the class be taught by one professor or by a team?

- How heavy is the reading for the course?
- Which readings are recommended and which are required?
- Is there a writing fellow (someone to help you structure your paper and arguments) for the course? If so, are meetings mandatory?
- Are make-ups possible for labs and sections?

A few freshmen are under the impression that, as long as they complete the course requirements, it doesn't matter who teaches the course; these students don't take into account the professor's teaching style, personality, and attitude when they select their classes. Unfortunately, they don't realize that a dynamic professor can transform a dry subject into an exciting one. Also, different professors may have different syllabi and requirements for the same class. In the majority of instances, those professors whose classes are overenrolled every semester are the most competent and interesting.

Catalogs containing critical reviews of classes can be found at most colleges. These catalogs contain student reviews for many of the courses offered. On the very last day of class, students are asked to fill out a questionnaire about the course honestly, rating certain aspects of the course—the instructor, reading material, writing assignments, examinations, and other information. These ratings are usually quite accurate. The students have no reason to sweeten the reviews since the instructor does not see them until final grades are handed in to the registrar. These questionnaires, however, are completed before the final exam and therefore don't take it into account.

Although the course information you obtain from your faculty advisor and the critical review is important, it cannot replace advice from upperclassmen. Most upperclassmen are very happy to help you decide on a satisfactory schedule. If you have a peer advisor, find out what courses he took, what he thought of them, and what he recommends. Upperclassmen can also be invaluable sources of old class notes, tests, and texts.

WORKLOAD

It is extremely painful to start a course, only to realize that the work is too much for you to handle. Many students let their pride get in the way and continue struggling until midsemester when they drop the course, exhausted. If there is a class that causes you an inordinate amount of difficulty, decide early whether you can academically, emotionally, and physically survive a semester of it. In some disciplines you may need a firmer foundation before attempting an advanced course. For example, Shirley, a student enrolled in a pre-med chemistry class, spent the first week of the semester trying to understand the beginning chapters of the text. She felt very depressed because she believed she was not intelligent enough to understand the concepts. After much crying and self-denigration, she decided to drop the course and take it next year after auditing it in summer school, where she hoped to strengthen her background. She was lucky; she decided on a strategy early in the semester.

Most college classes require more reading than the average high school course. When you schedule classes, you should not select

more than two with extensive reading assignments. Below is a general guideline for determining a course's degree of difficulty by its reading load. This guideline does not apply to hard science courses. With liberal arts courses only one reading of the material is necessary in order for the student to become acquainted with the main ideas. In many science courses, however, the material cannot be fully appreciated or understood without rereading. Of course, you will have to use your own discretion when assessing the reading loads for classes; factors such as type of reading material, student's interest level, and size of print must be taken into account.

Pages of reading per week	Difficulty level
250 and up	heavy
150–250	medium
50–150	light
under 50	gut (easy)

INTRODUCTORY VS. UPPER LEVEL COURSES

Introductory courses (those that are prerequisites for everything else) contain a disproportionate number of freshmen. Most of your classes during your freshman year will be intros. These low-level courses give students an opportunity to sample different fields of knowledge. Jennifer, a freshman, was told by her faculty advisor that neural science was a fascinating field. She had never heard of the subject before and was not sure what topics it encompassed. She decided to take the introductory level course and found the class thrilling. Three years later, she is applying to medical school with a concentration in neural science.

Introductory courses usually cannot be avoided, because they serve as prerequisites for higher-level courses in the department. If, however, you feel that you have had a sufficiently strong background in the subject to warrant your exemption from it, talk to the chairman of the department.

Some students wrongly take classes without first completing the prerequisites and do remarkably well. In most instances, though, upper-level courses (those with very high course numbers) are incomprehensible if you lack the necessary background. Sometimes, however, prerequisites are not as relevant to upper level courses as you might think; in some cases, they are used to limit enrollment.

Upper-level courses are usually filled with juniors and seniors who are concentrating in the subject. It is not a good idea to take these courses as a freshman unless you have extensive background in the subject. The upperclassmen in the advanced classes have already adjusted to the rigors of the college world, putting you at a disadvantage from the very first day. Introductory courses are full of naive freshmen like you. Therefore, it is best to save the advanced courses until sophomore year.

Advanced courses (especially in your major) look good on applications to graduate and professional schools. Admissions committees won't look too favorably on a transcript filled only with introductory courses because it shows no focus or depth. Just because a course has an impressive number attached to it doesn't necessarily mean it is difficult. There are plenty of easy upper-level courses; they're just hard to find.

EASY COURSES

Easy courses in college are called "guts." Why is this? Maybe because you think with your stomach instead of your brain. Guts are usually taken by students who need a light fourth or fifth course, or who want to increase their grade point average (G.P.A.). When I was a freshman I thought that guts were for students that could not handle the academic rigors of college. Wrong! Guts are for everybody. Never think that because a class is reputed to be easy, it does not have something to offer you academically. Marty took a course called Business Management 12. It was considered a gut, and roughly 500 students took it each year. When Marty graduated, he started his own successful company; he now considers Business Management 12 the most valuable course of his undergraduate career.

Some professors change the requirements and structure of their courses after they learn that students consider it a gut. It is, therefore, very important that you know exactly what the course entails. Every year students at one college signed up for Geology 5 (Rocks for Jocks) believing that it would be a gut. One semester the professor changed his grading criteria. He made it quite easy to pass the class but very difficult to get As and Bs. Those students who took the class in hopes of raising their G.P.A.s were sorely disappointed.

Courses that require laboratory work should never be taken as guts. In addition to class time, you'll spend an average of about three hours a week in lab and will probably have to turn in laboratory reports. This is a lot of time to spend on a class that you intend to breeze through.

Each person has his own particular talents; what is a gut for one person might not be for you. If, however, you talk to many students and constantly hear that a course is easy, then it is safe to assume it is simple. You should look at the reading material, the syllabus, and the old exams to make your final decision.

Many students don't take guts because they think that they will make their transcripts less appealing to employers and graduate and professional school admissions committees. This is true only if the admissions committees and employers know that the courses you took were guts. Usually introductory courses are perceived as lacking focus and being easier. Another way outsiders know your courses are guts are if they have really fluffy names like The Comic as Literature or Cowboys and Indians. There are, however, plenty of professors teaching upper-level courses (with impressive titles) who are very lenient graders. Why take a difficult course for the sole purpose of making your transcript look good? The admissions officers won't even know the course was difficult and that Prof. So-and-So of Art History 2000 is as hard as nails. Take the very difficult courses only if you: a) are required to do so, b) are truly interested in the course, or c) know the professor is a Nobel Laureate or president of the university and therefore has a name that will carry weight. For years now colleges have been thinking of adding information on the official transcript about the grade distribution in each class. Until this idea is implemented, however, follow my advice.

SCHEDULING

It is not advisable to have two lab, section, or class times overlap, even by five minutes. If you have a test in one of those classes, a loss of five minutes can mean the difference between a pass and a fail. Do not assume that you will finish lab early or that your section leader will end ahead of time. It is more probable that most of your classes, sections, and labs will run overtime.

Your final exam schedule is an important factor to consider when you are choosing your classes. The college semester is much shorter than the high school semester, and final exams always seem to be lurking right around the corner to cause you endless nights of worry and test anxiety. Ask your professors for the dates and times of finals. Because final exams can constitute as much as two thirds of your grade, some students choose their courses and sections according to the dates of the exams. They try to select their courses to allow the maximum time before and between finals. These students do not realize that the final exam schedule should be only one factor in choosing courses.

Here are some helpful suggestions for scheduling courses:

- Do not have more than three hours of classes in a row.
- Schedule a lunch hour every day.
- Do not allow labs, sections, or classes to overlap.
- Do not schedule your classes because you want a free day during the week.
- Do adhere to the deadlines for dropping/adding courses and grade changes.
- Do see your academic and peer advisors.
- Make sure that your finals do not overlap. If they do, talk to the professors whose exams conflict.
- Schedule enough credits so that you are not put on academic probation!
- Ascertain that the class meets at a reasonable time.

See page 47 for a sample schedule.

ADDING COURSES

Some courses have limits on the number of students who may enroll. Limits often reflect a shortage of classrooms, T.A.s, or lab spaces. You will realize quickly that it's impossible to get every class you want. If for some reason you are denied a seat in a limited enrollment class, there are still some things you can do as last resorts.

Weekly Schedule

	Mon.	Tues.	Wed.	Thurs.	Fri.	Sat.	Sun.
9 AM	Russian Lit		Russian Lit		Russian Lit		
10	Read Russian Novel	Studio Art	Read Russian Novel	Studio Art	Read Russian Novel		
11	Political Science	Read Russian novel	Poli Sci	Read Russian Novel	Poli Sci		
12 PM							Brunch
1	Lunch						
2	Go To Library and Research Poli Sci Paper	Inorganic Chem	Russian Lit Section	Inorganic Chem	Chem Lab	Soccer Game	Buy Groceries
		Read Russian Novel	Go To Bookstore	See Prof. Smith			
3	Sci Paper	Poli Sci Section	Read Mystery Novel			Write Chem Lab	Study Poli Sci
4	Intramural Soccer Practice				Rest	Write Chem Lab	Study Poli Sci
5	Dinner						
6	Read Poli Sci	Study Chem	Outline Poli Sci Paper	News-Paper	Draw Weekly Art Project	Read Mystery Novel	Chem Study Group
7							
8	Study Chem		Study Russian Lit	Study Chem		News-Paper	
9		Read Poli Sci Text					
10							News-Paper
11	Edit Stories for School's Daily News-Paper	Mystery Novel	News-Paper	Read Poli Sci	Movie	Semi-Formal Dance	
12 AM							
1							

One girl at Brown University wanted to get into an English class so desperately that she went to the class every day even though the professor told her that the class was full. After she attended the class for a week, the professor finally asked her for her add/drop form so that he could admit her. Another possibility is to tell the teacher that you really want to be in the class and that you are thinking of majoring in the subject. Above all, you must be persistent.

Adding a class after the second week of the semester can be very difficult. You will have many hours of lecture notes to copy and plenty of homework to make up. Some instructors even schedule tests for as early as the third week of classes. Further, after the second week of classes, most schools charge add fees. However, it is generally still safe to add a gut during the second and even third week.

4

Professors and Teaching Assistants

You probably never thought about it, but reaching the rank of professor is quite a harrowing and involved process. Unlike high schools, most colleges rank their teachers according to seniority and academic achievement. The faculty positions in ascending rank are assistant instructor or teaching assistant, instructor, lecturer, assistant professor, associate professor, and professor (or full professor). For the most part, instructors and lecturers are real-world professionals such as C.P.A.s and M.D.s employed by the university to instruct students in their specific fields. Teaching assistants are graduate students working on their doctorates who get financial support in return for teaching introductory courses and sections. After earning their Ph.D.s, graduate students start as assistant professors. After about five years, assistant professors who have done good work are promoted to associate professors, a title that confers tenure—the right to the position on a permanent basis. A tenured professor can't be fired except under extreme circumstances (e.g., proof of academic or personal misconduct or bona fide faculty cutbacks by the university caused by serious financial problems); the position is secure for life. Tenure protects professors from political pressures so that they can be free to pursue all fields of scholarly inquiry.

Tenure is often awarded on the basis of the number of books, articles, and other scholarly works published by the professor. This is why some professors put emphasis on their research at the expense of their students. It is a matter of survival.

CHOOSING A PROFESSOR

It is very important to consider the professor when choosing courses. Some freshmen are under the erroneous impression that it is of little consequence who teaches the course. Don't make this mistake. Upperclassmen know that the professor can make the class interesting or boring, the material easy or difficult, your grade an A or an F, and your life fun-filled or utterly depressing. Thus, it's worth taking special care to choose a class with the right professor.

Because Christie needed to increase her grade point average by a few tenths of a point in order to renew her scholarship, she decided to find a professor who would give her the best possible grade for her efforts. She, however, knew that easy professors and easy courses aren't necessarily matched; you're just as likely to find an easy-marking professor teaching a course chock full of difficult concepts as to find a hard-marking professor teaching a remedial course. Because you select an easy-grading professor doesn't mean you are goofing off or wasting your parents' money. It just means that you are getting the best grade possible for the work you do.

During the first week of school, Christie looked through the course catalog and made a list of those classes that looked interesting. She then read the course and teacher evaluations, paying careful attention to what students wrote about each of the professors. Comments like "This professor gives good grades to 90 percent of the class" or "This professor will make your life a living hell" helped her narrow down her list of possibilities considerably. To further uncover her professors' grading quirks, attitudes, prejudices, and methods she asked upperclassmen for their opinions on each professor. You can be sure that upperclassmen know who the easy markers and hard markers are.

She then sat in the professors' smaller classes so she could get a good idea of their personalities. In a small discussion group, Christie was able to see how each professor interacted with the students.

One professor she observed spoke in a weak voice that tended to trail off, a trait that often indicates leniency. She also noticed that he never knocked anything a student said, no matter how inane. When she talked to him after class and during his office hours, he told her that he rarely failed anybody and he didn't like to give grades lower than B. Bingo!

CULTIVATING A GOOD STUDENT-TEACHER RELATIONSHIP

Your professors will play a major role in your college career and your life afterwards. By the tone of the recommendations and letters of reference they write to graduate school admission officers, summer-job employers, and fellowship and scholarship committees, they help shape your future.

Thus, it is to your benefit to learn how to get along with your professors. The first step in getting on your professor's good side is to use the correct title. "Doctor" or "Professor" is the safest and most proper form of address for instructors past the graduate school level. Often teaching assistants ask to be addressed by their first name. If they don't specify, however, call them "Mr. . . ." or "Ms. . . . ."

To foster a good relationship—or at least a working relationship—with your instructors, do the following:

- Attend class regularly, and be prompt. If you must interrupt the lecture because of your tardiness, don't forget to apologize to the professor after class. For an in-depth discussion of attendance, see Chapter 5.
- Participate in classroom discussions. When you remain quiet, your professor comes to one of three conclusions: 1) you don't understand the material, 2) you aren't prepared, or 3) you don't care. Rarely will a professor permit a student to remain quiet during the discussion; you will very likely be called on to answer those questions for which there are no takers. So be sure to volunteer during each session. Don't, however, interrupt the discussion with vapid remarks for the sole purpose of participating; you'll be best

remembered for the foolish statements you make. Chapter 5 gives more tips on how to stand out in class.

- Be a hard-working, caring, and motivated student. Professors enjoy teaching students who want to learn.
- Stick around after class to ask the professor questions and to discuss the lecture material further. Not only does it help the professor get to know you, but it also gives you the opportunity to learn from the questions other students ask. In addition, in the minutes prior to the start of classes, some professors become friendly with their students by chatting with them about sports, current events, and campus happenings; it wouldn't hurt to arrive early and join in on the conversation.
- During class, nod, smile, look thoughtful, and listen intently and approvingly to what the professor has to say. This positive feedback gives the professor confidence and lets her know that you are paying attention. Don't, however, smile and nod constantly throughout the hour like a simpleton.
- Compliment your professor when she does well. If you thought the lecture was especially stimulating or enjoyable that day, let your professor know. She will appreciate a compliment like, "I really found today's lecture interesting and I'd like to learn more." Caution: Give only compliments that are sincere. Professors can distinguish the sincere students from the apple shiners.
- Make eye contact with your professor.
- Write diligently, and at the end of the hour be the last to put your pen down. This behavior shows the professor that you think what he says is important. Professors like to think that you were so interested in what they had to say, you lost track of time.
- Have good classroom manners (e.g., listen intently to what your fellow students have to say and don't interrupt). All students want to look good in front of their professor. Everybody knows the smooth operators who will deliberately ask their fellow students for favors or help in ear shot of the instructor, knowing full well that their classmate will grant the request to look magnanimous.

Good classroom manners also include respecting your professor's classroom rules and instructions. Whenever my high school drafting teacher lectured and wrote on the board, he expected everyone to put down his mechanical pencil and pay attention. One student, eager to finish his drafting plate and be free

of homework, continued to write while the instructor taught. The teacher noticed his inattentiveness and, after yelling a great deal, gave him an extra homework assignment.

- Don't be a show-off. Some students think that they know more than the rest of the class, including the professor. Maybe they do, but they will soon find out that professors and classmates rarely tolerate students who talk down to them.
- Don't hesitate to talk to your professor if you have something important to ask or say. Remember to talk politely; no matter how unfair or infuriating your professor is, never never argue with him.
- Dress neatly, and look your best. Studies reveal that beautiful people are thought to possess other desirable traits (i.e., intelligence, popularity, sincerity, and happiness). Why not take advantage of this psychological phenomenon?
- Think positive. Negative attitudes beget negative attitudes.

- Investigate your professor's pet topics. More often than not, professors incorporate their favorite research topics into the day's lecture. Visit your college's library, and read the articles your professor published recently. Be able to discuss and ask intelligent questions about aspects of his current research. Your professor will be impressed and excited to find a student interested in the same area(s) of research.

WHEN YOU AND YOUR PROFESSOR DON'T GET ALONG

On occasion, despite the best of intentions and deeds, you won't get along with a certain professor. The signs of a deteriorating student-professor relationship range from the subtle to the obvious. For instance, does he:

- Constantly criticize you?
- Make you the butt of every joke?
- Ignore you when you talk to him?
- Often behave uncharacteristically gruff and curt when talking to you?
- Tell you he can't stand you?

Even though you probably won't be able to make the relationship work anymore, you should figure out the reason(s) for the conflict (Does the professor hate everyone? Is he just reacting to your own hostile attitude? Was it something you did or said?). If you can, you may be able to prevent a similar situation in the future.

Most professors take special pains to be impartial toward those students they don't like. Some, however, don't. So if you aren't being paranoid and do see the "I'm out to get you" gleam in the professor's eye, you have a few alternatives: a) talk to him, (b) take the class pass/fail, c) complain to the dean or the department chairman, or d) drop the class.

In most instances, talking with your professor about the problem won't do much good because first impressions, whether negative or positive, are usually lasting ones. I recommend changing your grade option to pass/fail. This can often make the situation more bearable, because you'll only have to worry about passing the class.

Unfortunately, pass/fail is not always a viable alternative because of the many rules, deadlines, and regulations governing its use. It may simply be too late to change your grade option.

If you don't want to or can't take the class pass/fail, you can try complaining to the head of the department. You can justifiably complain about a professor if he:

- Behaves in a deliberately hostile and rude manner toward you.
- Is constantly unprepared for class.
- Makes sexual overtures toward you.
- Grades objective exams unfairly or doesn't give you the grade your exam scores indicate you deserve.
- Gives his favorite pupils special attention, favors, and extra considerations.
- Doesn't know the material.

Most likely, complaining won't change your situation because the chairman will be reluctant to do anything drastic against a colleague. Your complaint will only alert the university to a potential problem.

Although dropping the course is a drastic move, it is often the only solution to a bad student-teacher relationship. If the course is a graduation requirement, try changing your section, taking it another year or during the summer when another teacher is teaching it, or taking it at a different school (first make certain that you can transfer the credits).

THE PROFESSOR AS ADVISOR

In addition to teaching classes, doing research, and attending to administrative chores, professors counsel students on academic matters. This responsibility doesn't begin and end with scheduling electives and requirements. Professors can offer advice on majors, careers, graduate schools, summer and full-time jobs, and anything else that bears on your academic performance while in college.

Since an advisor can play a pivotal part in your life, it is important to find a good one. Upperclassmen can usually choose their advisors, but, for the most part, freshmen are assigned advisors. Don't settle for an advisor who doesn't have much time to devote to you and who signs your program card after giving your schedule only a cursory look to be sure you are fulfilling the school's requirements. If you are unhappy with your counselor for any reason, you should go to the departmental chairperson and request a professor who you know is a good advisor (a good professor may turn out to be an awful advisor and vice versa).

To help you in your search, here are some of the earmarks of a good advisor. A good advisor:

- Clearly posts office hours.

- Makes time for you and keeps appointments. When you have an appointment with your professor and she leaves you waiting for a long time, it is an insult. Whether the act is done consciously or unconsciously, it makes you feel very, very small and insignificant.

- Listens intently to your ideas before he gives you his.

- Doesn't hurry you or cut appointments short.

- Gives you privacy and his complete attention. He should close his office door so students in the hall can't overhear your conversation and should have his secretary hold all but his most important calls.

- Makes you feel comfortable. For instance, she sits in a chair next to you, not behind a big metal desk. She might also personalize the office with pictures of her family or her bowling trophies; this makes her seem more human and thus less intimidating.

- Doesn't give you pat answers or false reassurances. Some advisors want to be friendly with everybody; rather than be the bearer of bad news, they'll assure you everything is fine even when it is not.

- Follows up on the topics you talked about together.

Before you see your advisor, you should already know what questions you need to ask and what concerns you want to discuss. Once you get your answers, however, don't take them as absolutes. Seriously consider your advisor's suggestions, seek out the opinions of others, and then do whatever you feel is right.

5

Attending Classes and Taking Notes

Some students think that they can skip the first day of classes and prolong their vacation because the first day is usually devoted to administrative rather than academic matters. I, however, am here to tell you that it is the most important day of the semester because:

- You will probably receive a course syllabus outlining the course's required readings, papers, quizzes, and tests. (Pages 40–41 list most of the questions which the syllabus should answer; if it doesn't, raise your hand and ask.)

- Even if you are preregistered for a class, many professors start a new class list that includes only those present.

- Often course announcements and syllabus revisions made during the first day of class make the class more or less desirable. Should you change your mind on the basis of these changes, you will still be able to drop or add, since it is early in the term.

- The most desirable sections and discussion groups fill quickly.

- Your own observations, feelings, and biases about the professor's teaching style and general outlook on the course and its material will help you decide early on whether or not to drop the class. (However, on the first day you will not be able to tell the witty professors from the deadheads because they'll all be putting on their best performance.)

▪ Some professors let the class vote on important matters, such as the books to be included on the reading list, test formats, and the deadlines for papers and homework. Every vote counts, and if you do not like the options you can always offer alternative solutions, formats, deadlines, and books.

IMPORTANCE OF ATTENDANCE

Most professors don't care about attendance as long as you finish all assignments and pass all the tests. For your own sake, though, good attendance is a must if you want good or even passing grades on your assignments and tests. When you miss a class you lose valuable information—notes and announcements pertaining to quizzes, exams, papers, and projects. Statistics show that those students who attend classes regularly get the best grades. If you are enrolled in a class, lab, or small seminar, attendance is taken every day and is usually reflected in your grade. Some professors of small classes even limit the number of cuts allowed (usually three is the limit), and if you exceed this number you fail regardless of your grades. This might seem infantile, but it is the professor's prerogative to make up class policy.

The best advice is simply, "Don't cut." However, sometimes even the best of us miss a class. Most students cut classes for the wrong reasons (i.e., they're too tired or too lazy or they want to start the holidays early). There are, however, two instances in which cutting is allowable: when you are too sick to attend and when you need the time to finish a paper or study for a test. If you do miss a class, don't ask the professor to tell you what you missed; he is not going to repeat the lecture for you and the last thing you want to do is remind him of your absence. As soon as possible, get the notes and handouts from a friend who writes neatly and legibly. If you delay, you might forget to ask. Don't wait until the day before the exam to ask for the notes; your friend will also need them. Moreover, the missed day's notes might be pivotal to your understanding of the following lecture.

I recommend getting two different versions of the notes from your classmates so that your information will be more accurate and complete. When you have the notes, don't just photocopy them, write them out by hand. The physical act of recopying will help you to understand and remember the material.

When you know that you will be absent, ask your friend or neighbor to take extra-legible notes for you that day. Often, borrowing notes from your neighbor is a good way to make a friend.

College courses cover much material in very little time, and if you miss more than a week or two of classes you will be hopelessly lost. Therefore, if you must be absent for a prolonged period during the semester, you should talk to your professor or dean and perhaps consider withdrawing for that semester.

Often students must be absent on the day of an exam. If you have to miss an exam for any reason, you should give your professor advance notice if possible. In the event you can't reach your professor, leave a message with his secretary. Sometimes an unforeseeable illness or event occurs on the very day of your test. Most professors won't cause you undue grief about this as long as you bring a doctor's or dean's note attesting to your whereabouts, condition, or emergency. Otherwise, your absence might not be excused and a zero could be averaged into your grade. If at all possible, try your hardest not to be absent on exam days, because missing the test can cause you and your professor a lot of extra problems.

Make-up exams are graded on the same curve used for the original test; some professors purposely make their make-ups extra difficult to discourage absences and keep everybody honest.

LATENESS

If you are late for class, sneak in on tiptoes. It is always better to show up late than not at all. Don't, however, make it a habit; professors resent the disturbance your tardiness causes. Directly and/or indirectly, your professor will count it against you. Some professors limit the number of latenesses allowed before your grade is affected. If, however, your professor constantly lectures past the hour and makes you late for your next class, talk to both professors to at least make them aware of the situation.

Note: Usually professors reserve the beginning of the lecture for class announcements. So if you happen to be late, remember to ask a friend to fill you in on the few minutes you missed.

CLASS PARTICIPATION

In small discussion-type classes, participation is usually mandatory and will be factored into your final grade, sometimes accounting for as much as fifteen percent of your grade. Few professors will flunk a student who clearly tries to put his or her best foot foward in class discussions. If you come to class prepared, you shouldn't be afraid to speak up and share your knowledge. I suggest that you volunteer to answer any questions to which you know the answer, because if you remain silent your professor will call on you to respond to the one for which you don't have an answer. If, however, you are still too shy to participate in class, talk to your professor; he might take your shyness into consideration when he determines your final grade.

Here are some suggestions to help you stand out in class:

- Be prepared with good questions before going to class.

- Sit in front to make sure you keep eye contact with the professor and let the professor know that you are taking notes diligently.

- Make it a habit to contribute twice during each discussion period. It is preferable to be the first and last to talk. However, if you are not adequately prepared, do not make any comments; you might inadvertently reveal to your professor your lack of preparedness.

- Make insightful comments, and pose intelligent questions. Don't relate personal stories that lead nowhere or have no relevance.

- Appear genuinely enthusiastic about the lecture.

- Don't dominate the discussion in a rude manner, dwell on the obvious, or talk down to others.

- Talk to the professor after the lecture.

Note: You should follow these suggestions right from the beginning of the semester since it is very difficult to change a first impression!

Warning: Some professors teach by asking questions. This means that everybody in class is assigned a seat and the professor, who has a seating plan in front of him while he lectures, calls on people at random. The point is to scare students into doing the readings on time and thoroughly. Since the professor knows your name because of the seating plan, he can and often does put marks next to the names of those students who answer the questions incorrectly or not at all. I strongly advise you do the readings for courses that are taught in this strong-arm manner.

TIPS FOR TAKING A+ LECTURE NOTES

Lecture notes are absolutely essential in college unless you possess a photographic memory. It is a mistake to underestimate the value of taking and studying class notes. Consider Eric, who had to study for a midterm in geology. He didn't go to class often and didn't take notes when he did. He, however, knew the textbook down to the last footnote and thought his superior knowledge of the textbook would earn him an A. Eric received a B on the midterm because one fifth of the test's questions were based on the lecture material. Furthermore, some of the information given during class contradicted or otherwise updated information in the text. Of course, questions about this information popped up on the test, and only those students who went to class got the right answers.

In many classes your lecture notes will be the most important study tool, more so even than your textbook. In order to determine how important a certain class's lectures are, you must first examine your professor's lecturing habits. Do your instructor's lectures (1) follow the text and assigned material closely, (2) concentrate only on information ancillary to the textual material, or (3) dwell only on the major or tricky points of the assigned readings? If your professor's lectures fall into either category 1 or category 3, then the text is just as important as the lectures. Category 2 lectures, however, will be more important than the text.

Here are some tips for taking great lecture notes:

• Do the assigned reading before class. If you read the chapters that correspond to the day's lecture beforehand, you'll be better able to understand the lecture and organize your notes.

• Listen, don't just hear. It is easy to hear, but it takes concentration and effort to listen. When you listen, you absorb the material and relate it to previous information stored in your memory.

• Sit in the front. This will stop you from daydreaming, reading the newspaper, or talking to your neighbor for fear of being caught and publicly humiliated. An added benefit is that some lecturers watch the front-row students in order to gauge their speed of delivery. Furthermore, when you have reason to talk to your professor, he will remember your face.

Note: On very rare occasions the class is seated alphabetically. If you find yourself seated in the back of the room, complaints of eye, hearing, or concentration problems will often be honored.

• Sit under good light but not near the dream-inducing windows.

• Don't slouch. Slouching makes you sleepy and leads to sloppy notes.

• Don't sit next to a friend or someone you are madly attracted to. Neither will help your concentration. In all probability, you and your friend will whisper and pass notes; if you just happen to sit next to an attractive somebody, you will constantly be tempted to steal glimpses of him or her throughout the hour. On the first day of my freshman math class, I sat next to a very handsome student, and I became so nervous I didn't even realize that I spelled my first name wrong on the attendance sheet.

▪ Write neatly and legibly. Your notes will be a pleasure to study later.

▪ Use a pen that flows easily or a pencil that doesn't smudge.

▪ Use a good sized (9 × 11) spiral notebook. Looseleaf binders, besides being too large and clumsy, cause pages to fall out easily.

▪ Have a separate color-coded notebook for each course. In college, unlike high school, you will have just a few classes each day; if you use separate spiral books for each course, you will carry only what is necessary each day. Different color notebooks should be used for each course to aid in identification.

▪ Put the proper date on each page of notes.

▪ Paste the course outline on the inside of the front cover of your notebook for quick reference.

▪ Make your notes interesting. Don't just underline important words and phrases—draw arrows, stars, doodles, asterisks, or ex-clamation points next to them. Another way to call attention to important words is to put them in boxes or circles or use all capital letters. Vary the letter sizes for headings, subheadings, and sup-porting ideas and examples. If something is unclear, don't hesitate to put a big colored question mark near it as a reminder to ask the professor about it. Colors, drawings, and symbols serve as memory cues for you when you have to study your notes in the future. Some students use different color highlighters for main ideas, supporting facts, opinions, and tricky points. However, I don't recommend this because it takes too much time to do, and you will be hard pressed to remember what each means.

▪ Use shorthand as often as possible. Some professors spew out noteworthy information so fast your hand will cramp halfway through the lecture. What to do? One suggestion for those students who do not know any formal shorthand or speedwriting system is to devise your own shortcuts. Make use of technical symbols and standard abbreviations. In addition, you can devise your own ab-breviations by eliminating the vowels in a word, using only the beginnings of lengthy words, and adding "s" to abbreviations to show plural.

Note: Remember that the purpose of your shorthand is to make note taking faster and easier while preserving readability. Therefore, it is best to abbreviate only those words that are very long because their truncated versions will be easier to recognize. Make sure that your made-up abbreviation cannot be mistaken for another word that would make sense in the same sentence.

Some technical symbols you may find helpful are:

&	and	/	ratio
+	plus, and, positive	‖	parallel
−	minus, negative	∧	insert
@	amount, the amount of, at	∴	therefore
f	frequency, frequently	÷	divide, division
#	number, amount	×	multiply
$	dollars	=	equals, equivalent to
¢	cents	≠	unequal
?	question	≅	approximately
!	take note	>	more than
*	important	<	less than
( )	parenthetical	∞	infinity, unending

Standard abbreviations include:

cf	compare	re	regarding, referring to
eg	for example (*Note:* for speed, omit periods from abbreviations.)	Q	question
		A	answer
ie	that is	↓	down, decreasing
c/o	care of	↑	up, increasing
lb	pound	H_2O	water
c, w/	with	min	minimum
w/o	without	max	maximum
avg	average	etc	and so forth
		ok	okay

You can also abbreviate words by eliminating vowels (pblm for problem, indvl for individual, gvt for government) or using word beginnings (assoc for association, bio for biology, chem for chemistry, and prof for professor).

Add "s" to the abbreviations to form plurals (+ s for plusses, stats for statistics, govts for governments, and cfs for comparisons).

• Never, never alternate note-taking with a friend. The physical act of writing the notes in your book aids in memory retention.

Moreover, your friend might take skimpy notes on a topic because he or she knows it thoroughly; you, however, might never before have encountered the topic.

- Prepackaged notes are not to be used in lieu of but in addition to your own notes. There is no substitute for taking your own notes.

- Don't rely on your tape recorder for notes. Batteries have a propensity for going dead at the most inconvenient time. If the batteries do survive the hour, you will be lucky if you pick up half of the lecture between all the coughing, whispering and paper rustling. Unless you have a video camera, you'll also miss the information the professor writes on the board. If after all this you still insist on taping the lecture, remember to ask your professor for permission first.

- If the lecture is disorganized, don't try to organize it during class. Spend your class time copying down as much as possible; there will be time afterwards to organize your notes.

• Write down as much as possible. During class, professors often give examples, tell anecdotes, and recall stories that are tangentially tied to the day's topic. Don't follow the majority of students, who think such digressions are ancillary, and put your pen down. Take a second and note the essence of the professor's digression; you'll be thankful when it appears on the next test.

• Copy everything the professor writes on the chalkboard. The information must be quite important for your professor to write it down; follow suit. In my sophomore chemistry class the professor scribbled some lengthy reaction for making methane. A few diligent students copied the reaction down while the rest of us daydreamed, not even considering the possibility that it could be on the next test. You know the rest of the story.

• Copy lecture notes the way they are said. Do not put rules, principles, definitions and other main ideas in your own words; your paraphrasing might change the meaning.

• Be aware of your professor's hand signals and voice inflections. They may give hints as to the amount of importance she gives to a certain topic.

• Put a special mark (i.e., a star or asterisk) next to those ideas, concepts, topics, or points the professor spends an inordinate amount of time covering. This is another hint as to what she considers important.

• Listen for organizational cues and buzz words and phrases. Some cues and buzz phrases to remember are: "Notice that," "The basic idea is," "Now this is important," "Remember that," "The important thing to remember is," "To sum up," "Take note of," "The second reason for," "I can't stress . . . enough," "What I noticed is," and "Another consideration is. . . ." When you hear your professor preface a sentence with a buzz phrase, pay attention and be ready to write down what follows.

• Don't leave the classroom before the professor finishes talking. Those students who pack their bags at the end of the hour while the professor is still lecturing miss valuable information, information that they will, in all likelihood, be responsible for on tests. Furthermore, many professors consider it rude.

- Leave some space in the margins of the pages for your own notes, interpretations, and thoughts.

- Look over your notes right after class. This will refresh your memory. If you can't manage to look over your notes, at least make sure that your notes are complete, readable, and understandable before you leave the classroom.

HOW TO READ AND TAKE NOTES FROM YOUR TEXT

Textbooks, assigned readings, and handouts, unlike pleasure books, require you to take notes. Here are some suggestions to help you get the most out of your reading:

- Read your textbook as fast as you can. When you read slowly your mind tends to wander; before you know it you have finished the page but have no idea what you read. Don't mouth the words with your lips or read out loud; you slow your reading speed.

- When you are reading your text, always keep a pen, a highlighter, and your notebook nearby. This makes it easy to jot down and/or highlight important points.

- Read the summary first. It should give you a general idea of the chapter's contents. However, don't read the summaries in lieu of the chapters; summaries never have enough details to adequately prepare you for exams.

- Don't skip the introduction. It will probably answer important questions such as: Why am I reading this chapter, book, handout? In what historical context did the events occur? What have critics said about the book, author, theme, plot, or main characters?

- Skim the chapter before you read it. Look at the headings, sub-headings, italicized phrases, lists, illustrations, captions, tables, graphs, charts, bold typed words, and bulleted sections. Skimming helps you locate the important points in the chapter so that you can organize your thoughts and notes better when you actually do read it.

Note: You will not be able to skim a good novel because there are too many important plot and character clues hidden throughout the prose.

▪ Read to understand. Although you will be able to pass some tests by rote memorization alone, most will require a thorough understanding of the course material. Comprehension requires an immense amount of energy, especially for inherently difficult concepts, so, after each page, take a few seconds to ponder what you just read. Before you go onto the next page, be sure you understand everything you just read.

Professors know which topics require some mental gymnastics to understand. You can bet those difficult topics will be on the test to ensure that only those students who took time to understand the tough stuff will get the As.

▪ If, after pondering, you still don't understand something, pencil in a question mark at the top of the page as a reminder to ask your professor or teaching assistant during class or office hours to clarify it. Don't hesitate to write in your textbooks—most campus bookstores will buy them back anyway.

▪ Highlight important ideas, concepts, axioms, theorems, opinions, etc., with a yellow marker. Highlighting makes you remember the material better because you have to read it twice to underline it. On your first reading, you should highlight everything and anything you think is important. It is always a good idea to read your assigned material a second time in order to take notes. If, however, you don't have enough time to reread the material in its entirety, you should at least read the highlighted portions again. Don't be afraid to over-highlight; when it comes time to study it is always better to study a little more than a little less.

Some students use a ruler to underline important concepts. I advise against this because it takes too much time. Just underline freehand.

Note: I suggest using yellow highlighter because it is the easiest color to read through.

▪ Write your own comments, diagrams, ideas, opinions, thoughts, conclusions, and specific questions in the margins of your texts. You will understand more information when you scribble in the margins because it forces you to interact with the material in a mental, physical, and even creative way. In addition, your notes will serve as memory cues later when you have to review the chapter.

- Note where the lecture and the text differ. Often professors update textual information or disagree with something the author wrote. Write down and remember these divergences! Questions pertaining to them will be on the test, and only those students who went to class and took notes will get them correct.

- Don't copy your notes word for word from the text. By forcing yourself to paraphrase what you just read, you will remember it better. The only exception to this rule is that some definitions, axioms, and theorems must be copied and studied verbatim to preserve the exact meaning.

- Answer the study questions you find in the text. Usually there are questions either scattered throughout or at the end of the chapter. Many times professors use text questions verbatim on exams; students who didn't answer the text questions will kick themselves for losing such easy points.

6

Studying

College, like any job, requires a concentrated effort to complete. You must put in a certain amount of time on a regular basis. Since your college classes will take only a few hours each day, you'll probably have more free time than you would if you were working. Many people, however, find college more hectic than the real world; the problem is how to structure your free time effectively. The answer is to create a weekly and a daily schedule. Write the former on a calendar hung in a conspicuous place in your dorm room and carry the latter in an appointment book you keep on your person or in your bookbag.

Schedules are a must. Those students who keep schedules become more efficient and motivated in their studies because they always know what needs to be done and by what time. Schedules drastically reduce the probability that you will forget and/or mistake deadlines; if you adhere to the schedule you won't experience the anxiety of discovering that the test you thought was next Friday is in actuality tomorrow! When you finish an assignment and cross it off your list, you feel a sense of power because you are accomplishing tasks that lead to a goal. The fear of losing this sense of power will motivate you to complete more tasks.

A schedule gives you direction, saves time, and takes only roughly five minutes to create. See page 47 for a sample schedule. Below are some points to remember when budgeting your time:

• Reserve time in your schedule for extracurricular activities, social commitments, and personal responsibilities. Your schedule isn't only for academic matters. You'll need to put in your other commitments as well so that you can better decide how much free time you actually have and how to use it most productively.

• Let your schedule reflect your natural body rhythms. If you are most awake during the evening and sleep through the morning, plan to study during the night. During the afternoon students usually feel low on energy; save that time for doing errands that require little mental exertion, or take a nap.

▪ Be realistic when forming your study goals so that you will be able to adhere to your study plan. Unrealistic study expectations often go unfulfilled. Students become frustrated and often return to their former unsuccessful study methods. A week after you implement your study plan, reevaluate it and revamp it if necessary.

▪ Stay ahead of your assignments. This might be one of the most important pieces of advice I can give. You should finish all your assignments, readings, and projects a week ahead of their due dates. By doing this, you will not only be able to follow the lectures better, but in case an unexpected commitment or problem (i.e., sickness) prevents you from studying, you won't be hopelessly lost in class. If you don't take this precaution, a common cold can put you behind in your coursework by more than a week, spelling academic disaster. It's best to start jumping ahead of your academic responsibilities in the beginning of the semester when you have few commitments to honor and relatively little work to complete. Doing so will give you an edge on your classmates, who will be partying hard in an attempt to prolong the vacations. You'll be better able to prepare for reports, exams, and projects because you won't be rushed at the last minute.

▪ Don't study right after dinner. Most people feel sleepy after eating a big meal, because blood is concentrated in the stomach to aid digestion. Taking a nap is like putting money in the bank. Sleeping doesn't waste time; it reserves energy that can be used at a later date.

▪ Don't wait until you're in the mood to study. There are so many exciting things to do in college that you will rarely be inclined to study. Studying requires discipline. Otherwise you won't be able to sit for hours reading, memorizing, reviewing, and pondering a subject you hate.

On the whole, students don't do well in classes they dislike. Therefore, in order to do well, I recommend you try to make those dry studies more enjoyable. Psych yourself up before studying.

▪ Plan to study the most difficult subjects first. Steve had a calculus test one morning. Early in the evening the night before the test, he started redoing those problems in the textbook that the professor

LEARNING BY OSMOSIS

had assigned for homework. He didn't start to study the lecture notes and sample problems until after midnight. He knew he hadn't understood the solutions when the professor explained it in class. Unfortunately, Steve realized that he still didn't understand, but it was too late to call a classmate or the teaching assistant. Furthermore, his head ached and his eyes burned because he was tired.

▪ **Study at the same time every day.** When you study on a regular basis, your body falls into a routine and you reduce the amount of warm-up time needed.

Caution: In high school, teachers gave surprise quizzes to discover and then scare those students who didn't do the assignment(s). In contrast, college professors seldom bother with surprise quizzes; they expect their students to be responsible enough for their own education. Nevertheless, some professors do give pop quizzes every now and again, and although these quizzes won't figure prominently in your grade, they can mean the difference in borderline cases, so it helps to be prepared.

• Set aside enough time to study for tests. Have you ever realized late at night that you don't have enough time to study adequately all the material for which you'll be responsible on tomorrow's test? If so, you know how valuable it is to study without time constraints. Below you will find a *rough* guideline for the number of days you should plan to study for each type of exam:

once-a-month exams—three or four days

quizzes—one or two days

midterms and finals—a week

Of course, the exceptions (and they are numerous) to these guidelines depend on the particular student's abilities, the difficulty level of the test, and the amount of required readings.

• During each night's study session, study dissimilar subjects back to back. This prevents interference, the phenomenon whereby your memory of one subject interferes with your learning of another, similar subject. Thus, you shouldn't study two similar courses, like Spanish and Portuguese, consecutively, sandwich in a science, history, or art course.

• Reward yourself. After each study session, take a break and do something that will make you happy (e.g., read a few chapters in a mystery novel, listen to the radio, or eat a snack). Don't reward yourself if you didn't complete the day's scheduled assignments.

Warning: Don't watch TV in between studying. You will be tempted not to return to your studies. Furthermore, there is evidence that those who watch TV and then study aren't as effective or efficient in their studies as those who don't watch beforehand.

YOUR STUDY ENVIRONMENT

Do you remember when you could listen to the radio and/or watch TV and eat a snack while completing your high school homework in the middle of the living room? Well, those times are over. College coursework requires intense concentration; there will be very little if any busy work. In order to pay attention to your homework in college, you will need the right study environment.

Sit at a large desk in one corner of the room facing a blank, off-white colored wall with your head bent over, back straight, and right leg intermittently bobbing up and down, sit in a thinly cushioned chair complete with arm rests and a high back. Keep the temperature at a crisp 68 degree temperature. The room should be well-lit and quiet except for the drone of a fan somewhere and the occasional rustling when you take your hourly break to look out the window. Keep your desk clear except for a few highlighters, pens, pencils, and a bottle of cold water.

This is an ideal study scenario? First of all, the room is quiet, with few distractions. This by itself is not always ideal, because some people find that their minds wander when they are in total silence. The humming fan in the background provides "white" noise, which helps some people concentrate. Studies have found that cool temperatures also aid in concentration, and some students need to drink cold water to stay awake. The cushioned chair provides only enough comfort (thin cushion, arm rests and high back) so that the reader doesn't become stiff or sleepy. The lighting in the room is also conducive to studying; it doesn't shine directly on your book, producing a glare, nor does it shine in your eyes and cause eye fatigue. The blank wall in front of you and the big clear desk are also free of distractions.

One hazard students face is that they spend most of their time sitting, which can lead to poor circulation. You can improve your circulation when you sit by bobbing your leg up and down. This helps circulation by making the heart pump blood to all parts of the body and having the blood return to the heart by the contraction of voluntary muscle (i.e., the calf muscle and thigh muscle) around the veins. These contractions squeeze the blood up through the veins to the heart. So although a continuous shaking of the leg is often seen as a symptom of St. Vitus's Dance or some other nervous disorder, an occasional bob of the leg can prove beneficial.

The study environment can be an out-of-the-way place in the library, a student's dorm room, or even a study lounge. Each place can be an ideal study environment under the right conditions.

Although studying in your room is very convenient, it affords too many distractions—friends unexpectedly visit, sweethearts telephone, neighbors party in the hall. Freshman dormitories are also notorious for being loud at all hours. The situation is further complicated since most freshmen have a roommate, who will probably be on a totally different study schedule.

Many students who find they can't concentrate in their room study in the library. There are usually few distractions; you'll have nothing to do but study. In order to reduce your warm-up time, however, I suggest you study in the same place in the library every time so you can get to work immediately.

When I study in my room, I am always a bit anxious because I feel like I'm missing all the fun and excitement going on outside my door. In the library, however, I am surrounded by quiet studious students, whose mere presence allows me to concentrate. Misery likes *quiet* company. (There is usually a noisy floor or section of the library where students socialize and form study groups. People usually need a relatively quiet study environment; some students, however, find they can still study amid the commotion and excitement. You'll have to decide which is best for you.)

Studying at the library, however, has its disadvantages. Unless you bring all your textbooks to the library, you'll be limited in what you can study. Returning from the library at night can be inconvenient as well as dangerous. Walk home with a friend; there is safety in numbers.

I like to study in the dormitory lounge because it is quiet and not far away. I can return to my room for books when I want to change subjects or topics. Besides being free of auditory distractions, the room is usually sparsely furnished (only a few chairs and tables), with no decorations, and provides very few visual distractions. Unfortunately, the lounge may not be an option for some students; some colleges, lacking the necessary dormitory space, do not have student study lounges.

To prepare themselves psychologically for an exam, some students study in the room in which the test will be administered. Studies have shown that when you are tested under conditions similar to those experienced while learning the material, the likelihood of recall is greater because people tend to associate certain facts with the environment in which it was learned. This may work for you.

WHAT TO STUDY

Many times your professor will let you know the test's format ahead of time; he should tell you what types of questions, information, and thinking strategies will be emphasized. If he doesn't, you should feel free to ask him about any of these concerns. When professors start talking about an upcoming exam, they sometimes inadvertently reveal some of the questions and/or topics. So ask your questions and carefully note the professor's answers.

Most students do not know what to study for their first exam. I recommend study overkill; study your lecture notes, textbook, handouts, outside readings, and old exams thoroughly. In essence, study everything! Even though you might have a good idea what will be on the exam, you don't want to be unpleasantly surprised. After the first test, you'll know your professor's teaching and testing styles better and can study accordingly.

OLD EXAMS

Procuring a copy of a previous year's test can mean the difference between a C and an A, because old tests give you an idea of the information your professor considers important. Once you look at the exam here are some questions that you may be able to answer:

1. What topics does your professor like and stress? Does your professor have favorite questions or problems?
2. What kinds of questions (i.e., multiple choice, short-answer, essay, true-false, etc.) are used on the exam?
3. Are the questions pulled primarily from the lecture, the text, or a combination of sources?

You can often get old exams from friends who have already taken the course. Save your old tests, homework assignments, and textbooks to trade or give to your friends and classmates. Fraternity and sorority members often save their old course material for their brothers and sisters. Some departments keep folders of course tests and syllabi for student review. Many professors even put their exams from the previous year on reserve in the college library.

(After each semester, professors update the library's file of reserve exams, and the older exams are removed. Therefore, if you know which courses you will be taking in the future, ask for the reserve folder in the library and photocopy the old tests. When you do take the course, you'll have one or two extra tests to use for practice.)

If this is your professor's first time teaching this course, try to locate the tests given by the course's previous instructor; the material will be similar, and the practice will be good preparation for your test. If you can't find any of the course's old tests and your instructor refuses to divulge his test's format, get a copy of his exams from his *other* courses; this will give you a few clues for your test. Usually professors become fond of certain test formats and question types.

To ensure that nobody has an advantage because of popularity or fraternity membership, some professors don't ever give back exams. In this case, you can ask upperclassmen what they remember about the exam's format and material emphasis.

Few professors alter their tests radically from year to year, most simply update them or add information. Those professors who use the same tests every year usually fall into one of the following categories:

1. Older teachers. Older people are often set in their ways and reluctant to change.
2. Long history of teaching the course. Such teachers have a collection of questions that they usually put on their exams.
3. Lazy or uninterested in the class. Some professors don't invest much time or energy in teaching, preferring instead to devote themselves to research.

Old tests are very effective and legitimate study aids. If there are old tests for your course floating around campus, wheedle a copy from somebody. Otherwise, you'll be at a decided disadvantage during the quiz, monthly exam, midterm, and/or final.

HOW TO STUDY

Study Groups

A study group is a gathering of a few friends and classmates to review, discuss, and quiz each other on course-related material. Only study in a group if everybody has done the required reading and is prepared to contribute. For example, Becky realized that there wasn't enough time left for her to read all the novels required in her 19th-century English literature course. She got together a few of her classmates and formed a study group to discuss the important aspects of each of the five required novels; she chose the students carefully so that there was at least one person in the group who had read each required book.

Don't permit students who haven't read the material to join your study group; you'll spend your time explaining the obvious and slowing the group down. Keep the group to a minimum of two or three people—if you add more participants, the group will likely turn into a bull or gripe session or a party with megamouths and class clowns all vying for attention!

Group study sessions should be used for review and/or for understanding the finer points and details of a topic. Members can also use the time to fill in the gaps in their class notes. If, however, you haven't done the bulk of your studying (i.e., read, understood, and memorized the basic points, premises, and opinions of the readings), don't study with a group! You'll get more done by studying alone.

The group study session lends itself to certain subjects more than others. This method isn't as effective for chemistry, physics, and math courses that require students to do practice problems as it is for humanities and soft science courses for which a round table discussion can be an effective study tactic.

On occasion, professors and teaching assistants conduct and organize study sessions where questions are answered and course material is reviewed. Come prepared to learn and ask good questions—you'll be surprised by the wealth of relevant information you'll find.

Memorization

Although rote memorization won't play as big a part in your college career as it did in your high school and grammar school education, it will still be important for good college grades. You'll need to memorize facts, names, formulas, theories, and opinions in your humanities and science courses. Once you memorize the information, you'll be better able to form your own conclusions, opinions, and theories based on what you learned and memorized. Below you will find a number of practical memory tricks, aids, and facts:

▪ Study in a cool environment. There exists evidence (from experiments conducted on goldfish) that a cool room temperature (about 68° F) aids retention. I once heard of an eighteenth-century poet who allegedly swore that the cold air sharpened his thought processes. Every morning he had his servants lock him up nude in a

cold storage room and instructed them not to let him out of the room until he had finished a set number of pages of verses. (This is how I wrote this book.)

• Your recall is significantly worse after an interval of wakefulness than after an equal period of sleep. Experiments indicate that if you are finished studying for the evening you'll remember more in the morning if you go to sleep right away than if you stay awake. Rest reduces the amount of interference you experience and helps prevent you from freezing up during the exam.

• Study the most difficult topics first. People have enhanced recall for the first and last things they studied, heard, or observed, during a particular period. Additionally, you should work on the hardest material in the beginning of your study session, when you'll be the most alert.

Note: When you study, spend some extra time on the material that came in the middle of your previous study session. Otherwise, your recall of this material will be weak.

▪ Associate the information with as many senses as possible. Most instances of forgetfulness result from failures of retrieval and not of storage. By encoding the bit of information by its sound pattern and letter sequence, you double your chances of later dredging up its memory trace.

▪ Memorize facts in short periods of about twenty minutes each. By taking breaks every twenty minutes or so, you prevent fatigue and facilitate maximum recall because your nervous system has enough time to transfer the information from short-term storage to long-term storage.

▪ Understand and learn the material well. You'll have better retention and recall as well as command of the information if you understand the logic behind it. For instance, if you are asked on a test how to derive a certain formula but don't remember the specific steps, you'll be able to derive the formula by working backward and applying logic if you understand the thinking and principles involved.

▪ Don't allow distractions when you study. If you study with television, noise, or music, you won't be able to learn or recall well. Worry and preoccupation also interfere with learning and memory storage. If you are too concerned about some personal problem, stop studying; on a piece of paper write down all your options, decide which one provides the best solution, set a tentative date for the execution of your solution, paper clip the paper to your weekly or daily schedule, and then forget about it. It is also advisable to avoid studying after intense outbursts of emotion or excitement.

▪ Tie in new information with the old. You'll learn the new information better and faster when you associate it in your mind with well-established and remembered information.

▪ Make your textbook and lecture notes and study sheets as colorful, vivid, odd, and interesting as possible. Be creative—draw pictures, graphs, and stars; highlight, underline, and circle words. This will make the dry material more memorable. The bits of odd and interesting information won't need this treatment because they'll automatically stand out and become part of your store of knowledge. For example, in the senior year of high school I reread my biology textbook in its entirety; I remember one fact in particular because I found it odd and interesting, yet logical: The temperature in your big toe rises by one degree when you go to bed. Now I know why I stick my toes out of the blankets at night.

• Dispel negative attitudes. When you lack interest or dislike a subject, you will have difficulty learning and recalling the material. Make yourself like it.

• Don't study similar subjects in succession. For instance, squeeze an hour of German between an hour each of inorganic chemistry and organic chemistry to avoid having the learning of new material hamper your recall of the old.

• Use study tricks to remember course material. Mnemonic devices are little tricks designed to make memorizing easier. For my American Civilization course, I needed to memorize the six sources of folklore (newspapers, weeklies, paperbacks, almanacs, illustrated works, and theater) for a fill-in-the-blank test. I took the first letters of each word and created this silly story—Nasty Willie Ate a Ticklish Porcupine and got Indigestion. Try to make your stories funny, exaggerated, or in reversal of the traditional or normal. By making up an interesting or colorful story and forming its corresponding mental picture, you'll amuse yourself while you learn.

Depending on your letter set, acronyms can sometimes be easier to form. For example, I had to remember the five basic criteria for judging the descriptions in child behavior studies: reliability, objectivity, validity, replicability, and sample representativity. I formed an acronym by taking the first letter from each of the words, rearranged them (they didn't have to be memorized in the same sequence in which they were presented in the textbook), added a "y," and came up with **"Sorry, V."** Add and subtract letters to make meaningful and nonsensical words.

• Practice, review, read and repeat aloud. Much of what we learn is forgotten in the first twenty-four hours after studying. Only information that is used daily eventually gets transferred from short-term memory to long-term memory. Your memory is like a muscle—with use it becomes more powerful and more efficient. Experiments indicate that overlearning material reduces forgetting significantly. A few days before the exam, make up a study sheet of all the formulas, theorems, definitions, facts, and graphs you'll need for your exam. Quiz yourself by covering up the information and seeing if you can recall it without looking. Carry it around with you for the next day and study it any chance you get—in the cafeteria waiting for dinner, on line at the bookstore, or before class. By studying everywhere and anywhere, you'll be better able to recall the information in all types of environments because you studied in many places. When you practice memorizing only in ideal conditions (i.e., quiet, comfortable, moderately warm places), you may not be able to recall the material during actual exam circumstances.

You should also read aloud the notes and information to be memorized. When you read silently, sometimes you miss words. Reading aloud ensures that you don't read over something important, because you are forced to form every word. It also associates the material with two senses, sight and sound, making recall twice as likely.

Another good way to memorize is by explaining or paraphrasing the information out loud to yourself, a friend, or an imaginary audience. By teaching, you'll also learn. You'll be astounded to realize all the questions that you didn't think about and can't answer.

Cramming

Even the most carefully laid plans can go awry, and few students go through college without ever pulling an all-nighter. Cramming throughout the night is physically and mentally painful. Some students can't endure this torture because they don't have the physical and emotional stamina. For most procrastinators, however, cramming is an integral part of their college experience; for them, one night of agony means the difference between an A and a C.

For most students, cramming often means learning information for the first time. Cramming sessions, however, should be used for *reviewing* the material at the last minute. Don't make them your first exposure; for all but the easiest courses this is academic suicide. I recommend a last-minute review of course material because during a twenty-four-hour period you forget most of what you studied, and it is better to be informed and tired than uninformed and rested.

Prior to the night before the exam, you should have already:

- Read all the required readings (preferably twice) and highlighted the important information. Ideally you should have taken notes on your textbook, handouts, and other assigned readings. Nothing is too trivial to study and write down so that you're not shocked to see questions pertaining to the book's graphs, tables, and even footnotes.

- Done the problems, questions, and review exercises at the end of each chapter and in the study guide that accompanies your textbook.

- Attended most of the lectures and asked questions about those things you didn't understand.

- Copied your friends' notes for those days you missed lecture.

- Completed all assignments pertaining to the material covered on the upcoming exam.

- Gone to a review session if your professor or teaching assistant hosted one.

- Reviewed the course's tests from previous years.

In addition to the study suggestions I made in the other sections of this chapter, here are some additional tips for surviving a cramming session. (These tips are equally applicable to regular study sessions when you aren't pressed for time.)

- Don't take naps in between cramming. You might be too tired to get up, let alone resume your studies. I find short rests of approximately twenty minutes invigorating. I have, however, had some scary moments when I woke up to find I overslept.

▪ Make up a study schedule for the night. This will help you stay organized and directed, which will in turn reduce your anxiety and worry.

▪ Reread the highlighted portions of your notes at least three times and read everything else once. The tests in most courses will stress the information contained in the lecture notes, because 1) your professor might not remember the material in the textbooks because he read them so many years ago, 2) most professors feel a need to personalize their courses, and 3) by putting lecture material on the test, the professor forces students to attend lectures.

You should read everything over at least once so that you will see the material as a whole and not just a collection of parts. The mind functions better when it possesses a complete picture for recall.

▪ Take special note of graphs, tables, charts, pictures, captions, and footnotes. Expect to see questions about them on the exam. They can also serve as memory cues for other bits of information.

▪ Limit your intake of coffee, tea, cola, and caffeine pills. Controlling your intake of caffeine will prevent your feeling jittery during the night. Don't do drugs like speed, amphetamine, or pot; not only will there be harmful mental and physical side effects (i.e., nervousness, jitters, and stomach ailments), but you also risk arrest by campus or city authorities and possible expulsion from college. A cold shower, brisk walk, and/or mild exercise will usually wake you up if you start to lose energy and fall asleep.

▪ Have protein-rich food available to keep up your strength in the wee hours of the night. Be careful. Try to stock up on low-fat and low-sodium edibles that are high in protein energy. Often students become depressed while studying late at night and overindulge on gooey, high-calorie snacks.

Tutors

Even after the most diligent studying, you may still not understand some of the concepts and information in a course. Your professor will have office hours each week for those students who want to ask questions. If your confusion can't be cleared up within a twenty-minute office visit, you might want to consider getting a tutor. Your professor or dean will be able to assign you a tutor, usually a student who took the class in a previous year and did very well. Most colleges provide students with tutors free of charge, so you have nothing to lose.

7

Taking Tests

It's an unfortunate fact of life that in college you will not be able to escape tests. You should figure on at least a midterm and a final for each course. For certain courses, you may be tested and quizzed more often or required to do a paper instead of or in addition to the exams. Since a significant percentage of your course grades will be determined by your performance on tests, you should be aware of some basic exam room strategies:

• In order to refresh your memory, do a quick review of the material before you go to sleep and when you awake in the morning. This will reinforce some of the information in your short-term memory; some will even be transferred from your short-term to your long-term memory.

• Eat properly beforehand. Tests are physically, mentally, and emotionally draining; you'll need food for energy. For long tests, bring a high protein snack that isn't messy or noisy. Avoid rich foods; you might become lethargic.

• Wear comfortable clothes. I can't understand how people can concentrate when their clothes are cutting off their circulation and preventing them from sitting and breathing.

• Bring a watch so that you can apportion your exam time wisely. Allocate more time to those questions that are worth more points. Students often find themselves rushed for time on difficult exam questions because they spent an inordinate amount of time on questions they found easy but that were worth only a few points. For example, you should spend around 12 minutes on a question worth 20 percent of a one-hour exam (.20 × 60 = 12). Leave yourself a few minutes at the end of the exam to check for spelling, grammatical, and factual errors.

• Arrive early. You'll be able to choose the most desirable seat (i.e., away from your friends, a talkative proctor, a drafty window, or a steaming radiator).

▪ Stay away from other students before the exam. They might unwittingly or wittingly psych you out. For example, ten minutes before the biology exam started, Alison approached her classmate Lucy and wailed, "I'm so worried! I've heard such terrible things about this professor's exams. I studied for weeks and I just know I'm going to fail." Susan, who started studying only a few days ago, became quite nervous and froze during the test.

▪ Upon receiving your exam, check it over for any missing or unreadable pages.

▪ Read and follow instructions carefully. Unless promised extra credit for your added efforts, answer only the required number of questions if given a selection of multiple-choice, short-answer, or essay questions from which to choose.

▪ Answer the easy questions first. This will give you confidence and refresh your memory in preparation for the harder, thought-provoking questions.

▪ Don't panic! Relax. Although you should be a bit anxious in order to keep awake and alert for tricks, some students experience so much anxiety that they freeze. The most common reasons for freezing are: 1) insufficient sleep, 2) physical and mental exhaustion, 3) too much caffeine or other stimulants, and 4) inadequate preparation for the test.

Those students who find themselves freezing up on an exam should talk to their professor or proctor. He might take it into consideration and allow you to go outside the exam room to take a deep breath of air or a drink of water. It also helps to find and complete a couple of easy exam questions to bolster your confidence. I usually feel less tense once I've answered a few questions. There is no better prevention against freeze-up than knowing that you studied the material thoroughly.

▪ When you don't know the answer to a question, take an educated guess and circle the question's number so that you can go back to it when you finish the exam. Try to answer each question when you come to it, because you may not have enough time to recheck. Furthermore, you waste time going back, rereading the question, and dredging up the appropriate memory traces.

- Your first guess is usually correct. Unless you experience a revelation during the exam, studies show that your first thought, guess, or interpretation is most likely to be correct. When you examine a question for the second time, you may not be able to retrace the mental processes that helped you arrive at your first answer. Instead you may follow a whole new line of thinking, one that is probably tangential to the question.

- Ask your professor to rephrase a question if you don't understand it. Sometimes professors and teaching assistants are willing to further clarify or expound on exam questions, especially thought questions requiring essays. Moreover, if you do understand the question but don't know the answer, often a hint or two from your professor will be enough to jog your memory. At the very least you might get some ideas with which to work.

- Write legibly. Your writing doesn't have to be superneat, just readable. Otherwise, your professor will be hard-pressed to decipher what you wrote, provided she is kind enough to try; professors have been known to mark sloppily written answers wrong automatically.

- Use all your exam time. Stay to the very end of the hour so that you can reread and check your answers for any errors. You'll make careless and costly errors if you rush to finish the exam. Besides, in the final minutes of the hour you might get a revelation.

- Don't leave anything blank unless your professor deducts for incorrect answers. Try to eliminate obviously incorrect choices, and make an educated guess; you have nothing to lose. In the rare case where the professor penalizes for incorrect answers, narrow your selection to a couple of plausible choices in order to increase the odds you'll guess correctly.

While taking the exam, don't watch, wonder, or listen to what your friends are doing (e.g., are they rapidly turning pages? did they finish the exam already? are they scribbling frantically or mumbling nervously?) This will only add to your anxiety.

In high school I took a calculus exam that had only four questions, each worth twenty-five points. I couldn't seem to do one of the questions, and with only ten minutes left in the exam, I began to panic. Luckily, I was able to calm down and concentrate, because I altered my way of thinking about the exam—instead of starting with one hundred points and just losing points thereafter, I started with no points and worked my way up. Psychologically I felt I was gaining, not losing! By thinking in this manner I was able to relax and concentrate clearly, enabling me to figure out the calculus problem correctly.

• While taking the exam, try to do the same things you did while studying for the exam. If you had coffee while studying you should have coffee while taking your exam. You never know how your mind recorded the information and what will serve as a memory cue.

OBJECTIVE EXAM QUESTIONS

Some types of objective exam questions you are likely to encounter are fill-in-the-blank, multiple-choice, and true-false.

Fill-ins

Students worry the most about this type of question. What if you just can't remember the word? You won't be able to guess as you would on a multiple-choice or true-false question. This type of question tests your recall, rather than recognition, of the material. Recall questions require you to remember the material. Unfortunately, although you studied thoroughly, a word, phrase, or definition may still elude you. This tip-of-the-tongue phenomenon can prove most frustrating. To dredge up the appropriate memory trace, go through every letter of the alphabet trying to find the first letter of the forgotten word; the first letter is often all the hint you'll need to remember the word.

Multiple-choice questions

Multiple-choice or multiple-guess questions might seem easy— you need only recognize the correct answer. Recalling the right word, words, or phrases for questions such as fill-ins may seem more difficult in principle than just identifying the right answer for a multiple-guess question. The difficulty with multiple-guess questions arises from the fact that the right answer is surrounded by others that are very similar. You'll have to be superastute to distinguish the subtle differences among the choices. To reduce confusion, read the question a couple of times and formulate an answer in your head before you look at the choices. Then systematically combine and consider the question with each of its options, eliminating obviously incorrect choices. Multiple-choice questions often have four or five options or answers; statistically, the first option will rarely be the right choice.

When you first read the question, circle qualifying words such as "most," "best," "every," "all," "sometimes," "never," "always," "equal," and "better." Beware of answers that include any of these absolutes: "none of the above," "all of the above," "always," "every," and "never," because few situations are so black and white.

True-false questions

Spend the least amount of time on the exam's true-false questions; they'll be worth only two or three points. When you get up to a question you don't know, just guess (there's a fifty-fifty chance of guessing correctly), put a circle or check near it, and come back to it later if time permits. Your professor will probably include more true statements because it is easier for her to copy sentences verbatim out of the text. Those statements with "rarely," "none," "sometimes," "generally," and "usually" tend to be true. Those questions containing "all," "only," "always," and "because" will in all likelihood be false. Furthermore, long statements tend to be true because it takes more qualifiers to make a statement true than false.

ESSAY QUESTIONS

Essay exams are generally considered more challenging than objective exams because essays require you to support statements, explore themes, integrate ideas, and form conclusions. When you take an essay exam, choose the essay question you can answer the best. Don't choose the most difficult questions just to impress your professor because you won't get any extra points.

After selecting the question you wish to answer, make an outline in your exam booklet. Outlines help you organize your thoughts and take only two or three minutes to devise. Once organized, you'll make fewer mistakes, and your first draft will look neat (this is important since you won't have time to recopy it). Don't erase your outline—if you don't have enough time to finish the essay, some professors will give partial credit on the basis of what you included in your outline. Also, jot little notes in the margins of your test as you think of things to include in your essay.

Your essay should include an introduction, body, and conclusion. Since some professors put a great emphasis on the introductory paragraph, it should clearly state what you intend to prove, examine, or show in the body of your essay. Your introduction should also define the terms, if any, you will use.

In the body of the essay, you will use evidence, examples, diagrams, charts, time lines, quotes, facts, and details to support your conclusion. Making specific points makes your essay seem stronger and more credible. Because essay exams are subjective, that is, open to the professor's interpretation, you should remember you are writing for an audience of one—your professor. In your essay, tie in what your professor talked about in lecture. If she stressed a certain point, topic, or fact in class and it is appropriate for the essay, include it. Whenever possible, use the specific vocabulary learned during lectures or while reading the handouts and text-books.

Some students pad their essays with everything they know about the topic. Be terse, especially on short essay questions not worth very many points; don't waste your valuable time writing irrelevant information, which will in turn cause your professor to waste valuable time reading it. If you can't think of anything else to write at the moment, don't add extraneous information. Instead, leave a few lines at the end of each answer so you can add more thoughts later.

An exception to this rule is this: If the question is vague and your professor won't clarify it, write whatever you think is relevant. You might just hit something. You should also throw in marginally relevant material if you don't know the answer but know something about the topic. For example, a common type of test question gives the name of a person and asks you to identify him or her. Your professor will be looking for specific facts. You and your professor, however, might not see eye to eye on what pieces of information should be included. In order to receive the maximum amount of credit, include as many major facts as possible, providing time permits.

A WORD ABOUT CHEATING

Because there is so much pressure to get good grades, some students may try to copy your exam answers. To avoid these students, sit in the front of the room, in the corner, or near a window. Current estimates suggest that 30 to 40 percent of college students are guilty of cheating at least once. By cheating, these students risk failure, suspension, and possibly expulsion; the exact punishment will probably be determined in accord with the guidelines set forth in your school's academic honor code (at Brown University, the code is

called Tenets of Community Behavior). The infractions will be recorded on the cheater's pemanent record, which will follow him or
her for a lifetime. Nothing is worth this risk.

In addition to copying from someone else's exam paper, cheating
includes:

- Taking a test or writing a paper for someone
- Having someone take a test or write a paper for you
- Plagiarism (see Chapter 8)
- Illegally using notes during an exam
- Sending and receiving messages during a test
- Accessing exam questions ahead of time

When you take your exam, don't sit next to your friend; if he or she wants to cheat off your paper, it will be hard to refuse. It is best to guard against this type of problem/pressure.

AFTERMATH

When you receive your graded exam, check to see that there were no mathematical errors made in tallying your score. Then examine those questions you lost points on and understand what you did wrong. Check your notes, textbook, and handouts for the correct answers. I find I learn material best when I get it wrong on a test. If after this review you believe your professor or teaching assistant graded your test unfairly, you can seek a reconsideration of your paper (see Chapter 8 on how to deal with this situation tactfully).

8

Writing Papers

Do you dread writing papers? If you do, you're not alone. Many college students feel overwhelmed by the volume of written work they have to produce each semester. Although the average college course requires students to write only one or two papers, when you multiply this by four (the number of courses you'll take each semester), the number becomes much scarier. It'll be even worse if you take a course with a professor who forgets his students have other classes and unmercifully requires seven long papers.

You should expect plenty of papers in English, history, political science, art history, and philosophy courses. Don't, however, think that by taking math, science, or economics classes, you can avoid papers; although these courses rely mostly on problem sets, tests, and quizzes, a few papers will be required as well.

Whether you have thirty papers, one paper, or a business letter due, you'll need to know how to research effectively and express yourself well on paper. This chapter will help you to write beautiful papers painlessly.

CHOOSING A TOPIC

You should start working on or at least thinking about your paper a few weeks before its deadline. Otherwise, you'll put it aside and forget about it, especially if it isn't due until the semester's end. Then you'll be crunched for time because of other papers, tests, and projects, and you won't be able to do your best. At the very least, you should have the research part completed way in advance unless you want to risk not finding the information in the library.

The great majority of professors give their students a free hand in choosing what to write about. Because finding a topic is the first and hardest stage in writing a paper, many students would rather dispense with this problem and have the professor suggest or require something; if these students enroll in a great many paper-writing courses, they will probably get a few professors who will limit them to very specific topics.

Take advantage of whatever leeway your professor gives you in selecting a paper subject. If you're permitted a choice, don't take the easy way out and automatically use those topics the professor throws out to the class as examples. Because many of your classmates will use them, there will be competition for the best research material, much of which will already be checked out of the library and/or reserved. Furthermore, after reading essentially the same paper over and over again all night, your professor will become bored and cranky. Try to personalize the paper; your professor will appreciate and remember you for relieving the monotony. Also, when you pick a very common topic, your professor will easily be able to compare your paper with all the others.

If you take my advice and decide to choose a unique topic, there are three factors you must take into consideration: (1) your interest and background, (2) the availability of information, and (3) your ability to cover the topic adequately.

Choose a topic that interests you. Not only will you be more likely to start the paper earlier, but you will also find the paper easier to write. People tend to work harder, better, and faster when they enjoy what they are doing. For instance, which paper would you write better and finish earlier—"The Superman Comic as Literature" or "Chaucer's Symbolism in *Troilus and Cressida?*"

If you're assigned a dry topic, try to develop an interest in it or at least look at it as a challenge. A positive attitude goes a long way toward putting together a good paper.

Some professors worry that students who are too involved with their topics will inadvertently write a biased paper or omit pivotal background information. Be aware of this pitfall. Explore both sides of the issue. If you're not sure whether to include something, have a friend read the first draft.

You'll be able to save additional time and energy by choosing a familiar topic. Does choosing a familiar topic lead to academic stagnation? Not if you choose a topic with which you are only tangentially acquainted. You only double your anxiety and labor if you pick something that requires a technical or extensive background you don't possess.

Once you get a general idea of what you want to write about, it's time to go to the library to narrow your topic. Once in the library, you may not find enough information on the subject to fill the required number of pages. If you chose an obscure, limited, or very specific subject, you may be forced to abandon it. You should have two backup topics already chosen to protect yourself in case of this eventuality.

The amount and kind of information you find should help you decide on the particular aspect of the subject you intend to investigate. After assessing the amount of information available, you may have to limit or expand the scope of your topic to fit your targeted paper length. For example, you shouldn't choose a vague and general topic like "The Dreyfus Affair" for a ten-to-fifteen page history paper; since a topic like this is far too broad (the library has at least twenty books devoted to it). You're better off with a very specific aspect of the topic, such as "Fear of Espionage: Catalyst for the Dreyfus Affair."

Although your professor doesn't expect your paper to be a scholarly breakthrough, she does expect it to have a thesis statement supported by facts, evidence, and data. Remember the good old days of high school and grammar school when you received good grades for book reports and textual summaries? Well, this type of paper won't cut it in college; you'll only court failure.

After you've chosen your research topic, talk to your professor about it. She might be able to make some helpful suggestions.

Before you meet with her, jot down any problems, questions, or concerns you have about the assignment.

USING YOUR LIBRARY

In all likelihood, your college will have more than one library. Many libraries are specific to certain subjects (i.e., science, music). You should visit each library as soon as possible since they will play a big role in your life; many college students literally live in the library. Find out which has the most comfortable chairs, the quietest atmosphere, the bulk of your course's reserved readings.

Once you have a few general ideas, go to the library and review the most recent card catalog entries, which will be computerized. The library computers are supereasy to use; they were especially designed for the computer illiterate. All you have to do is follow the instructions that appear on the screen. For each relevant book, encyclopedia, or article you find, copy down the title, publisher, date of publication, call number, and stack (floor) number on a 3×5 index card. Then find each source and note its relative importance on the index card. If the book isn't useful, keep its index card anyway, but label it "unsuitable" so that when you come across it again, you won't forget and waste time relocating it. Put all your index cards in alphabetical order; this will make it easier to write the bibliography.

If you start your research early, you'll have enough time to try other libraries in your area. Your local library won't have the most recently published resources, but for some topics, old books are just as usable. For example, for a paper entitled "Marie Curie's Influence on Modern Nuclear Medicine," you could use old sources for the background information on Curie's life, work, and achievements. Furthermore, if you have plenty of time (it usually takes a few weeks) and need another library's book, you may be able to request it through an inter-library loan; ask your librarian.

In addition to old books, your local public library will also have many encyclopedias and young adult and children's books available. Don't be afraid to use these books for preliminary research. They'll help you to fill in any missing details or background information quickly. Suppose you want to find out the particulars of Marie Curie's life for your paper on her influence on modern nuclear medicine. You could begin by reading a child's book on her; then, when you skim the adult texts, you'll have the necessary background to understand what you find.

Warning: Most of the information found in encyclopedias and children's books is common knowledge. Footnotes won't be needed. Don't include encyclopedias and children's books in your bibliography unless you quote these sources in your paper. Try to save your bibliography for your most impressive sources (i.e., journals.)

If you can't find something, ask the librarians. Not only will they tell you where to look, but most will also look with you. They can save you from hours of aimless searching.

THE STRUCTURE OF A RESEARCH PAPER

A research paper consists of an introduction, a body, and a conclusion. The introduction should be well written and succinct, since some professors assign grades without ever reading any farther than your first paragraph. So make it hook your reader! The introduction must include your thesis statement, a highly detailed sentence that directs your paper. Unfortunately, a thesis statement is often very very difficult to formulate.

How do you find your thesis statement. After collecting as many sources as possible, skim through them, reading the subheadings, introductions, and indexes. Start with the easiest and most general books first (i.e., encyclopedias and children's and young adult's books). Once you've collected information on your topic and skimmed through the material, you should be able to come up with a statement that you can successfully support, prove, and argue. If you already know your exact topic, just look it up in the index of each book; your statement should be specific enough that you don't need to read the books or articles in their entirety.

The body of your paper will be dedicated to supporting, defending, proving, and clarifying your thesis. In the beginning of the body, define the terminology you will use and present any necessary background information. Then argue your case. Present all your evidence, starting with the flimsiest and finishing with the strongest. Remember to include, analyze, and refute information that contradicts your paper's basic premise, supposition, or hypothesis. Show both sides of the issue; otherwise, you will be guilty of incomplete and biased research.

Like the introduction, the conclusion should be well-written and concise. It should summarize your thesis statement in a new way and take it a bit beyond.

ORGANIZING YOUR RESEARCH

As you skim through your research material, lightly underline in pencil any information you can possibly use in your paper. Copy each bit of supporting information (i.e., quotes, data, facts, and figures) onto a 3 × 5 index card. In order to readily identify the information's bibliographic source, code your cards by number or by color. These cards make it easier for you to organize and write the body and bibliography of your paper.

Once you have taken notes on all the pertinent information, it's time to write an outline, consisting of an introduction, a body, and a conclusion. An outline will give you direction and cut down on the number of times you rewrite and revise. Order your index cards so that they correspond to your outline. Now you're ready to start writing.

COMPUTERS

Once you've done the research for your paper and have an outline, you're ready to make a rough draft. You will find that at this step in the process, a computer or word processor will make your life much easier and your paper more professional-looking. Many students prefer to write their rough draft right on the computer so that they can then add, copy, and delete information with just a few clicks of the mouse. A standard feature of most word-processing programs is a spell-checker, which will alert you to any word that does not match any word in its memory.

Another advantage to using the computer is that it allows you to save information so that you will be able to work on your paper in bits and pieces over time. Computer disks can store a great deal of information in a very tiny space; I stored this whole book on a single 3½ inch diskette with room to spare. As you work, however, be sure to save your work every half page or so. Otherwise, all your work could disappear as the result of an unexpected power surge or an inadvertent touch of a key. In addition, if your work is on a hard disk drive, you should make backup disks, because occasionally hard drives get erased. In addition, if your computer is ever stolen, your hard drive, which is inside the computer, will also be taken.

If you don't already know how to use a computer or word processor, don't worry. Many computers and word processors are user friendly, which means they are specially geared for the computer illiterate. Consider Jason, who bought a computer from the campus computer shop. Although he had never used a computer before, he was able to set it up and learn enough of the basics of word processing to print out a paper that same day. In order to learn the fancier aspects of your word-processing program, you'll have to study the manual a bit more. In addition, your college will probably offer computer workshops and mini-courses.

An increasing number of colleges have computer rooms set up in different areas of the campus for twenty-four-hour student use. Since these computer clusters are usually very crowded, you will probably have to wait to use a computer and printer. Unfortunately, during reading period and exam time, when everybody has papers due, your wait could last for hours. Therefore, if you are planning on getting a liberal arts degree or taking a number of paper-writing electives, I recommend you buy a computer or word processor. Most campus computer stores allow students to purchase computers at substantial discounts. You might find your computer to be your wisest investment during your college years.

WRITING THE PAPER

With your outline, research material, and index cards close at hand, it is time to start writing. The actual writing and rewriting should be done over the course of a few days. Some students, however, insist on procrastinating and end up pulling all-nighters. Provided you're a good writer, it is still possible to hand in an acceptable paper under these conditions. However, if you're starting the paper the night before it's due without having done any preliminary research, you're in trouble.

No matter when your paper is due, you'll find these tips helpful:

- If you use a word processor or computer, save information every half page to guard against accidental erasure.

- Use quotes sparingly, and keep them brief. Try to use your own words whenever possible. Otherwise, your paper will be just a collection of other people's sayings.

- Vary sentence length. It becomes monotonous when every sentence has the same number of words (i.e., Jack ran up a hill. Jill followed after him. They both fell down. Unfortunately, they hurt themselves. What a terrible accident. You get the picture?).

- Omit from your paper all slang, contractions, and phrases such as, "I don't know but . . ." and "I think, suspect, or guess that . . ."

- Use vocabulary specific to your course to show the professor that you are immersing yourself in the coursework.

- Have reference aids, such as a dictionary, thesaurus, two-volume encyclopedia, and almanac readily available. Use an unabridged dictionary to make sure you don't miss the fine distinctions in meaning between words.

- Don't rely exclusively on Barron's or Cliff or Monarch Notes. They should be read in addition to, not in lieu of, their corresponding books. Use these notes only as a starting point for your research.

- Have coherent transitions between paragraphs. Your arguments must follow each other logically and smoothly.

- Make the paper one or two pages longer than the professor's requirements, provided there are no specific rules against this. Don't, however, pad your paper with unnecessary information, because it makes your paper look disorganized. Your professor will spot superfluous and redundant information immediately. If you're below the required number of pages, there are other ways of increasing the paper length (e.g., change the size of the letters or font, increase the margins, include charts and diagrams, add subheadings and subtitles, and place footnotes within the text instead of on a separate sheet at the end).

• Write the title paragraph after you've written the first draft of your paper. You'll have a better idea of what you actually proved, demonstrated, or argued once the first draft is completed.

• Don't be pedantic and use fancy words. You risk using them incorrectly and looking foolish. Using too many polysyllabic words usually indicates that you used the thesaurus too often.

• After finishing the first draft, leave it alone for a couple of days. Subconsciously, your mind will work on it. When you do return to your work, you'll have a new and fresh perspective.

• Have a friend proofread your paper for errors in punctuation, grammar, spelling, and organization. Another effective method for spotting errors is to read the paper out loud. Some professors don't take off for minor errors, such as misspelled words, but often they circle them in red marker. If your paper had many such tiny mistakes, your professor might only remember that she constantly had to put marks on it.

• If you need serious help with structuring your first draft, bring it to your school's writing center. If you ask your professor, he might be willing to look over your first draft and give you some thoughts on how to improve it. This also shows your professor that you are trying and didn't just put the paper together the night before. If you decide to do this, make an appointment early, because many other students will need help with their papers as well.

• Use proper footnote and bibliographic forms. If your department or university has its own guidelines, follow them.

• Don't pad your bibliography. Your professor will know that you couldn't have possibly read and used all those sources for your paper.

And now for the finishing touches:

• Never, never, never turn in a handwritten paper. Type it. With the advent of computers there is no good reason for a sloppy or handwritten paper. I still cringe when I think back to my freshman year, when I handed in an English paper handwritten—and in pencil, no less!

- Proof your paper for any grammatical, structural, or spelling errors. You must keep the number of mistakes to a minimum because they make your paper look unprofessional and sloppy. Pencil in only a few corrections. Professors tend to give higher grades to those papers that are error-free and neat because these little things show you care.

- Pick a catchy title. Look through the body of your paper for title ideas.

- Use good typing paper with 25 percent cotton content. It will not only look good; it will feel good. Don't use erasable bond or onionskin; the latter is too thin and the former causes the ink to smudge.

- Use a well-inked typewriter or computer ribbon. Your professor won't appreciate a paper with faint printing or a paper with blackened-in "e"s and "o"s.

- Put the page number and your name in the upper right corner of each sheet.

- Double space.

- Make a cover sheet. Here is how to set up the title page:

```
                          Title

              (centered and typed
               one third way down page)




          (aligned at        Your name
           right and         Course name
           typed two         Professor's name
           thirds way        Yesterday's date
           down page)
```

▪ Before you give your professor the original, make a copy of your paper. If you use a computer or word processor, just save your paper on the disk. This enables you to refer to the paper in the future and protects you in case your professor loses or misplaces your work.

▪ Don't paper-clip the pages together. Paper clips have a way of falling off. Place one staple in the upper left corner instead.

A NOTE ABOUT PLAGIARISM

Before starting your paper, make sure that you know the right format for referencing your sources. Every year many students are accused of plagiarism, the illegal use of someone else's information and ideas without giving proper credit. If you copy something verbatim, you *must* indicate that it is a quote. Furthermore, when you paraphrase facts, opinions, or ideas from a book, article, or other source, you must footnote the reference. A ten-page research paper will probably have upward of twenty footnotes, whereas an English paper of comparable length, full of your opinions and interpretations, won't need any. Knowledge that is fairly common also need not be referenced. For instance, the date of George Washington's birthday is common knowledge and therefore isn't footnoted, but the specific findings of a psychological study must be. Most of the time you won't be able to make a clear-cut distinction. It's safer to err on the side of having too many footnotes.

All too often, students fail to put in enough footnotes or any at all. If caught plagiarizing, you may be subject to failure, suspension, and expulsion, which might also prevent you from getting into a graduate or professional school. In addition, the publisher and author of the plagiarized material can sue you.

Some students are under the erroneous impression that they won't get caught. In reality, because professors have long memories and read extensively in their chosen field, they can easily spot plagiarized information. Sometimes it is especially easy for them; two papers may have the same exact plagiarized paragraph (an occurrence that is increasingly likely with popular topics). So if you find a paragraph in a text that is perfect for your topic, paraphrase and footnote it. Don't take unnecessary risks.

IF IT'S LATE

If at all possible, hand in your paper on time. Whether you have an extension or not, professors remember and resent those students who are always tardy with assignments. Once in a while, however, extenuating circumstances prevent you from completing an assignment within the allotted time period. Try to talk to your professor beforehand and get an extension; otherwise, there will be heavy penalties (some professors won't even accept late work, and others will drop a letter grade for every day late). Never just hand in a paper late without some kind of excuse. This only heaps insult on top of insult. Missing the deadline without an extension is the first insult; not caring enough to explain your disregard for the rules is the second. Explain to your professor that your computer malfunctioned and you lost everything or that you became sick with the flu and couldn't finish. Most will understand.

When you know that you will have problems meeting the due date, ask your professor for an extension well ahead of time. If you are the first one to ask, he will probably be more gracious. Don't ask the day before the paper is due; many of your classmates have already come up with all kinds of excuses and the professor will be moved only by the most desperate.

YOUR GRADE

Before you write your paper, you should find out the criteria your professor uses in grading papers. I knew of one philosophy professor who explained his grading system this way: "Provided all the papers are well thought-out and written, the longer ones will receive the higher grades. Twenty-page papers will receive an A, fifteen-pages a B, ten-page papers a C, and under five pages, an F." Other professors have different standards; some professors are especially impressed by papers that are beautifully written or well-organized or full of vocabulary specific to the course.

If your professor doesn't volunteer to explain her marking system, ask her about it. Suppose she won't talk about it or says something unenlightening. Since you don't want to wait until your paper is handed back to learn your professor's marking strategy, examine the relevant papers of a student who took the class some time in the past. Carefully analyze the reasons for the assigned grade, taking special note of the professor's comments. Ask the student for his opinions and ideas on the teacher's grading system. You should now have a good idea of what your professor wants. After you get your first paper back you'll have an even better idea.

ONE FINAL NOTE

Save every paper you write, electronically or otherwise. Not only will you need the copies in case your professors accidentally misplace the originals, but you might be able to reuse them, in whole or in part, for other classes. Furthermore, employers and graduate schools often ask students for writing samples. In the future, you might also want the papers in order to show another student what a particular instructor expects.

9

Grades

In our society, grades have become a tool for measuring a student's involvement in and comprehension of academic material. Grading is highly inconsistent; grading policies and standards differ dramatically from one professor to another. This, however, is something you will just have to face because nobody has devised a satisfactory substitute, although many have tried.

I cannot emphasize enough the importance of grades; they will be one of the most important and enduring aspects of your college experience. Like it or not, your marks determine whether you win honors, graduate, are accepted into graduate schools, and get employment offers.

Many college freshmen go into shock when they receive their first marks because they are often much worse than what they were used to in high school. Sometimes students who had straight As in high school barely make Cs in college. Some of the major reasons for this are:

- High school teachers give students more opportunities (i.e., tests, quizzes, projects) to boost grades than do college professors.

113

• Freshmen suffer from lingering symptoms of high school senior-itis.

• Colleges admit only those students who can do the work; high schools usually admit students from a certain area. Therefore, the competition in college is much keener.

• Unlike high school tests, those in college stress comprehension and application.

• Often courses are graded on a curve, which increases competition and puts a ceiling on the number of As allotted; it also guarantees at least a few failures.

• Assignments, projects, tests, and papers in college tend to cover more information in greater depth and at greater length than those in high school.

• College professors, unlike high school teachers, do not often offer students the option of doing extra-credit assignments as a way of improving their grades.

• Most of your academic work in college will be done outside the classroom; some students can't handle the increased freedom and responsibility.

Those students who fail a test or assignment should take time to evaluate why. Did you study properly? Did you apportion your time wisely? Are you involved with too many extracurricular activities? Is the class too advanced for you? If you still can't figure out why you failed, talk to your professor or dormitory counselor. It is critical that you find the underlying reason or reasons for your failure; otherwise, you may find yourself failing other classes and winding up on academic probation.

SCALES AND CURVES

You should always ask your professor whether she grades on a curve or on a scale. Most college exams are graded on a curve. This means that the professor will evaluate your test performance in the context of how well your classmates did. Ideally, there should

be an equal number of As and Fs and the same number of Bs and Ds. Implicit in this approach is the assumption that the majority of the class does average work, deserving a C. Those who do the best get an A, and those falling below a certain mark fail.

This method has two major flaws: 1) It fosters competition among classmates, and as a result, students hesitate to form study groups, share information, and lend notes, and 2) It is contingent on one particular class's performance. The 70 you receive on an exam might be an A in your class but that same grade on that same test might be worth only a B in another class.

Some professors grade students on a predetermined curve on which the cutoffs for As, Bs, Cs, Ds, and Fs are decided in advance of the exam. Under this system, everybody can get an A or everybody can flunk. Therefore, it is in everybody's best interest to cooperate in preparing for the exam.

GRADING OPTIONS

For those students who do not want to receive letter grades of A, B, C, D, or F, colleges offer the following grading options:

1. Pass/Fail (p/f)

Many students use the pass/fail option (in some schools it is called pass/no credit, pass/no pass, satisfactory/no credit, or credit only option) because, no matter your grade, anything above a D is recorded as a P on your transcript. If, however, you failed, an F is entered as your grade. Not all classes can be taken under this option; some professors don't allow students to take their courses p/f for fear the students will lose their incentive to learn and work only hard enough to pass. For this same reason, some colleges don't permit students to take required classes under this option. Furthermore, in most schools, pass/fail is not a choice for those students on academic probation.

If your school limits the number of times you can use this option, be savvy and take a class p/f only when:

- You know you don't do well in a certain subject but you have to take it.
- You are taking an especially difficult or heavy courseload.
- You feel like experimenting.

With the pass/fail alternative, no one need ever know that you really received a C in your Music 100 class!

The pass/fail option, however, has drawbacks. Colleges usually require students to file for this grading option by a certain date. If the deadline is too early in the semester, you might not have had any tests, papers, or projects in the classs by which to gauge your current and likely future performance. In this case, it is sometimes helpful to ask your professor about his grading practices. If your professor says, "I rarely give As," I recommend you take his class pass/fail if you are concerned about maintaining a high G.P.A. In addition, if you earn an A in a class you took for pass/fail, no one will ever know unless you ask your instructor to mention it in a letter of recommendation to go in your permanent file. Another drawback is that a transcript full of Ps doesn't look impressive to graduate school admissions officers, potential employers, or scholarship committees. So don't abuse the pass/fail option; only use it when it is necessary.

2. Audit

Auditing a class means that you attend lectures when you want and take the final exam. If you pass the final, your transcript will show a grade of Audit; students who fail have no mark recorded on their transcript. This option might seem attractive to you, but be careful, some schools do not give credit for audited courses. Furthermore, you can't use this grading alternative for your re-

quired courses. Because the audit option, like the pass/fail option, permits students to pass with the minimum amount of work, it doesn't look good on a transcript.

3.   Incomplete

Students who, for compelling reasons, are unable to complete the remaining assignments and tests in a course can receive a grade of incomplete and finish the coursework at a later date. Incompletes have saved many students from academic disaster; therefore, if you need an incomplete in one of your courses, talk to an instructor or dean who can grant your request. Some schools are very lenient in handing out incompletes; often the student and the professor decide on the deadline together.

Many students, however, take an incomplete in a course and then forget about it. Eventually, if they exceed the time allotted to complete the work, their grade of incomplete becomes a failure. You should finish the work as soon as possible to prevent this from occurring, as well as to avoid having the left-over work interfere with your other classes' assignments and to avoid having the course material become stale.

Unless you have the willpower to study for exams, write papers, and finish projects over vacation, don't take an incomplete.

4.   Repeat

What can you do if you didn't do very well in or even failed a course? Some colleges give students a second chance by permitting students who received a C, D, or F in a class to retake it and have only the second grade entered on the transcript. Be careful, though. Some colleges let students repeat only those courses they failed. To make situations worse, the final grade is the average of the two grades, so that the highest possible grade is a C.

Like the pass/fail and audit options, the repeat option is usually limited; many colleges allow students to use it only three times during their undergraduate career. Make use of it! It's a great opportunity to get rid of any blemishes on your record.

GETTING A GRADE CHANGED

If you have a legitimate reason for wanting your grade changed, you should make an appointment to discuss the matter with your professor or see her during her office hours. Be careful not to approach her about this matter in public; you might force her to make a hasty decision because she feels challenged.

The best approach for seeking a grade change on subjective exam questions and papers is politely to show your professor where on your exam or paper you think she overlooked or misunderstood something. Profess to having used an obscure interpretation or unusual approach to the question. Use these words because they won't put your professor on the defensive. Don't ask your professor to regrade objective test questions unless you can justifiably claim that the exam question was poorly worded or misleading.

If your professor won't budge but you still feel strongly about the exam question(s), your only and last recourse is to go to a dean or the departmental chairman. However, I don't recommend this for two reasons: (1) You don't want to antagonize your professor by going over his head; you might have future exams, papers, projects, or classes with this instructor, and (2) You won't get anywhere with your complaint because deans and department heads are very reluctant to meddle in the classroom policies, decisions, or opinions of a colleague unless they are blatantly wrong. So don't pursue this avenue unless you're quite certain never to come in contact with the professor in question again.

What should you do if you added all your marks and your final grade is borderline? Follow the same guidelines mentioned above but be sure to ask your professor before the grades are finalized which mark you will receive, because once it is entered on your transcript you have very little chance of getting it changed; your professor won't want to be hassled with the ton of extra paperwork granting your request will generate. Mention your class participation, provided you were assertive and insightful during the class's discussions; it might be worth a couple of extra points. If this doesn't work, then ask your professor if you can do an extra-credit assignment to improve your grade.

If your grade is especially important to you and you can make a good case, by all means try to get it changed, but don't expect much; most appeals are denied.

COMPUTING A GRADE POINT AVERAGE (G.P.A.)

Most colleges convert your letter grades and credit hours into numbers based on a four-point scale. Some schools use a five-point scale but for now we will concentrate on the four-point system; it will be easy to extrapolate the rules for the five-point from those for the four-point system. In addition, some colleges don't give varying credits to different courses, and instead assign equal weight to every course. The method for computing your grade point average under the noncredit system is very simple and can also be extrapolated from the method shown for the credit system.

The G.P.A. is calculated in the following manner: First convert your letter grades into the numerical value listed below. Then multiply that number by your credit hours to figure out your quality points:

Course	Grade	Numerical Value		Credit Hours		Quality Points
Anthropology 101	A	4	×	4	=	16
Medieval Lit 21B	B	3	×	3	=	9
Personal Nutrition	C	2	×	3	=	6
Basic Chemistry	D	1	×	6	=	6
Rudiments of Music	F	0	×	2	=	2
				18		39

Note: If your college uses +s or −s add .3 or subtract .3 from the numerical values accordingly.

Then divide the number of quality points by the number of credit hours to get your grade point average:

$$39 \div 18 = 2.167 \text{ (G.P.A.)}$$

This shows that you are a solid C student—a fact your parents might already know since some colleges send students' grades home addressed to parents.

10

Friends and the Campus Social Scene

Friends will play a pivotal role in your college education. Indeed, the quality of the friendships you form will often be the deciding factor in determining the success of your college experience. Friends will help you celebrate the good times, cope with the bad times, and prevent loneliness in between. On the flip side, friends are often the cause of much pain and sadness.

You must make a special effort to find a good group of friends. Choose your friends carefully because 1) they will have a great influence on your social, emotional, and academic development, and 2) people judge you by the friends you keep. For instance, if you associate with students who practice good study habits, you will probably develop similar habits. Furthermore, since you associate with the studious crowd, your classmates and professors will automatically assume that you too are studious.

As you choose your friends, keep in mind your priorities and the traits you value in a good friend. The next section on meeting people and making friends will help you have a large group from which to choose your best friends.

MEETING PEOPLE AND MAKING FRIENDS

Fortunately, you won't have to go very far in order to find good friends. Studies have concluded that your best friend will probably turn out to be your next-door-neighbor or someone else with whom you constantly cross paths. As a freshman living in a dormitory, your floormates will become your closest friends because you will constantly run into them, increasing the likelihood of finding that you have qualities and interests in common. This is why those students who live at home or in off-campus housing find it very difficult to make friends. If you live in a dormitory, don't get an isolated room in the basement or attic; try to get a room on the first or second floor, close to the kitchen, lounge, or stairwell, where you will have a greater opportunity to come in contact with other people.

In addition to living in a dormitory, there are other things you can do to meet new people and make friends. Whether you're a very outgoing person or just the opposite, these tips will help you:

- Make yourself accessible. Too many college freshmen just continue to socialize within their little circle of old high school classmates. Certainly you should keep your old high school chums, but at the same time you should try to meet new people and make new friends. Students who sit in their rooms studying all day and all night shouldn't wonder why they don't have any friends. Go out and try to make contact with as many people as possible each day! You'll make more friends if you:

- Attend classes and sections. Of course, your primary reason for going to class is to learn. Classes and sections, however, present a great opportunity for meeting new people. It is so easy to lean over to the person next to you and ask to see the syllabus or yesterday's notes. You might even be able to organize a study group.

- Position yourself in the classroom so as to maximize your chances of meeting others. Don't sit in a corner of the classroom room all by yourself. Sit in one of the front rows, near many other students. (As a bonus, students who sit in the front of the classroom tend to do better in class than those who sit toward the back and sides.)

- Eat in the cafeteria. Have dinner with your friends or just sit down with a group of people you've never met before.

- Study in the library. Your library probably has a mezzanine or some other equally open area where students socialize.

- Join an extracurricular activity. You will work closely with others who share your interests. Try to join an activity that will put you in contact with many people.

- Go to student mixers. You won't be able to meet anybody at a loud and dark frat party where everybody is drunk. If you want a real relationship or friendship and not just a quick fix, a quiet student get-together is for you.

- Now that you've surrounded yourself with people, make sure to talk to some of them. Force yourself to talk to at least one new person each day. Shyness pays no dividends.

• When you meet someone new, try to remember his or her name. If you have problems remembering names, try to associate the person's face and name with something familiar to you. For instance, if the person introduces himself as James Fox, you can associate his face with someone else named James. To help you remember his last name, just imagine a furry fox.

• Smile often. People want to be around people who seem happy and optimistic. By smiling, you convey a message of warmth and acceptance; people tend to like those who like and accept them.

• Be an open-minded listener. Freshman year is a very difficult time for many people, and they will be very sensitive to criticism. Even though you may try not to be judgmental, occasionally your tone of voice, facial expression, or body language will inadvertently betray your thoughts and feelings. Be careful.

FRATERNITIES AND SORORITIES

Another way to meet new friends quickly is to join a fraternity or sorority. By becoming a member of a Greek letter society, you automatically have a whole new set of friends.

The down side is that by joining the brotherhood or sisterhood, you might also be alienating yourself from some of your peers. If you spend most of your free time with your brothers and sisters, you may soon find that they constitute your social world. Furthermore, because of the party animal/dumb jock stereotype associated with Greek society members, some students won't want to know you. You might want to look into the reputation of the Greek societies on your campus; on some campuses it's considered cool to be in a fraternity, but on others it's just the opposite.

Suppose, however, you do decide to go Greek. How do you go about joining? The first step is to learn more about the individual fraternities (the local and national chapters) and their members. One frat might be called the football frat because most of its members are on the football team or the doper frat because its members are heavily into drugs. If a frat has been kicked off campus (denied college-owned housing) by college officials, be careful; you don't want to be associated with it. Because many of your classmates will automatically prejudge you on the basis of your fraternity's reputation, you should be careful which one you join. Don't just join for the sake of being a brother.

After you've picked out a few, you will have to take part in a screening process called rushing. On most college campuses, Rush Week starts sometime during the early spring. During the rushing period, you visit each prospective frat and meet the members. In order to receive a bid (an acceptance), you must receive the vote of every member of the fraternity. If just one brother votes against you, you will automatically be rejected. During open houses, be sure to chat with every frat member and try to make a good impression. They will in turn be on their best behavior and will shower you with attention.

While the other rushees engage in small talk, chug-a-lug beers, and play fooz ball, try to ask some penetrating questions about the fraternity and its policies. For instance, you might want to ask:

- What are the grades of the members? By associating with studious students, you will pick up some of their good study habits.
- What types of commitments are required? Some fraternities require new members to devise and implement extremely time-consuming projects in addition to the normal slop work of cleaning up after parties and get-togethers.
- How much are the annual dues? They can add up to hundreds of dollars each year.
- Where do new pledges live? Pledges invariably get the worst rooms in the house. Your room will be small and on the noisy first floor, and you'll probably have to share it with another student from your pledge class.
- What is the initiation process like? Unfortunately, some fraternities continue to haze their new members. They may even brag about their crazy or daring hazing process. Hazing, which has in the past caused students to become severely ill and even die, is such a problem that some states have even passed anti-hazing laws. Then why do fraternities still have it? Some studies have concluded that people come to strongly believe in a group or idea after having suffered and committed time and energy on its behalf. By making pledges experience some pain during the initiation ritual, fraternities expect to arouse intense feelings of commitment; they believe the pledges will feel even more compelled to justify and continue their involvement in the group. Cults use initiation rituals for very much the same reasons.

Since rushing is such a time-consuming process and since most fraternities hold their rush activities at the same time, you will need to focus your attention on a single fraternity. After you attend the Rush Days of a few frats and ask the members some of the questions suggested above, choose one frat and go to every one of its Rush meetings. The more frequently you attend the activities of a frat, the greater the opportunity to meet its members.

After Rush Week, the frat members will decide who receives bids. If you do get a bid, you might receive a visit from your new brothers in the middle of the night. This can be a noisy affair, since they will tramp down the dorm hall and into your room chanting.

If you accept the bid, you will become a pledge. As a new member of a Greek letter society, you can expect to go through an embar-

rassing initiation ritual about which you will be sworn to secrecy. Don't feel compelled to do anything you feel is wrong. Each year a couple of students die from hazing and hazing-related activities, and a greater number require hospitalization.

After you move into the frat house, you will be required to memorize the history and rules of the fraternity and participate in a special pledge project (e.g., building a new bar or helping out at a local community house), all of which will be very time-consuming. As a new member, you will also feel pressure to dress, speak, and part your hair a certain way. The people you socialize with, the sports you play, and even the courses you take will be expected to be in accord with the values of the house. You will have to give up part of your own individuality in order to conform to the group's expectations and standards.

Once you become a pledge, you will receive a few academic fringe benefits. For instance, older members will be able and eager to help you become better acquainted with the college system. Furthermore, your fraternity will probably keep folders full of old course notes, books, tests, quizzes, papers, and projects from its members. You will have access to these files.

DEALING WITH FRIENDS

Once you've made a few new friends, you will have to deal with them without losing your sanity. In addition to the golden rule, "Do unto others as you would have them do unto you," here are some other rules for dealing with friends:

Rule 1: Don't be upset when you find out that many of the people you thought were your closest friends in the beginning of the semester aren't really your friends later on in the year. At the start of school, everybody is a bit scared, and most students just cling to the first available person for friendship. As the semester progresses and students become more comfortable with their surroundings, they no longer need the security-blanket relationships. Psychological findings show that the differences among students grow as their college career progresses; attitudes and feelings change. Studies conducted on college students have revealed that freshmen start out quite similar in terms of attitudes, but by the time they become seniors there are marked differences among them. For example, freshman year Robbie and his roommate, Mike, were best friends. Sophomore year Mike joined a fraternity, and Robbie became a residential counselor, living with freshmen. By junior year, they weren't friends anymore and hardly had anything in common. Their experiences had drastically altered them.

Rule 2: Cultivating a good friendship is very time-consuming. Expect to expend time and energy on your relationships. Call, write, and visit your friends. Set aside time in your schedule to go to dinner or a movie with them. If you don't spend time with your friends, prepare to lose them.

Rule 3: The most enduring friendships are equitable ones. Both parties must feel that what they receive is in proportion to what they contribute to the relationship; otherwise there will be bad feelings on all sides.

Rule 4: Don't do anything that makes you feel uncomfortable just to keep a friend.

Rule 5: When your friend's behavior bothers or hurts you, speak up. Don't let negative feelings fester. Not only are you being unfair to yourself; you're also being unfair to your friend, who in all likelihood has no idea why you're acting so aloof, cranky, or curt.

Rule 6: Think the best of your friend and his or her actions and motives until you find concrete evidence to the contrary.

Rule 7: Share information about yourself. If you don't talk to each other about your feelings, beliefs, and attitudes about life, you won't ever be good, intimate friends.

11

Your Health

A HEALTHY ATTITUDE

Mental outlook is an integral part of overall health. A negative outlook can lead to a host of psychosomatic illnesses. For instance, sophomores often experience a slump, during which they lose interest in school, let their grades slip, and become dissatisfied and depressed about their academic career. The timing of this slump is tied to several factors: Sophomores tend to be overconfident about their academic and social abilities; join too many extracurricular activities, leaving them hard pressed for time, and feel anxious about choosing their course of study. The right mental attitude can be the first step in overcoming sophomore slump and going on to accomplish great things.

People who have a healthy attitude have definite goals and dreams they believe they can and will accomplish. They possess an internal locus of control, the belief that they are the overseers of their own destiny. Those students who have an external locus of control, who believe that outside forces control their fate, tend to: 1) receive lower grades in school, 2) be manipulated easily, 3) remain dependent on others, and 4) make less money. If you believe in yourself and your abilities, other people will, also, and you will find that your peers will want to associate more with you.

In order to determine your locus of control, choose which of the following statements you feel is more true.

- A person usually gets the grades he deserves. *or* All too often a student's efforts go unrecognized when report card time arrives.
- Average people can be involved in the political decision-making of this country. *or* Unfortunately, our country is run by a few, and nothing can be done to change it.
- Just because the course is closed doesn't necessarily mean I can't get in. *or* Once a course closes there isn't anything left for me to do about it.
- I alone decide what career I want. *or* Circumstances, such as market demand, will be the biggest determinant in which career I ultimately end up with.

Those people with an internal locus of control generally choose the first statement of each pair as true. If you have an external locus of control, here is a step-by-step guide to help you alter your perception of control:

Step 1: Set definite and realistic short-term and long-term goals for yourself. I find that I get more done and am not as easily sidetracked when I have direction. For instance, one of your short-term goals might be to get straight As this semester. Your long-term goal might be to get into one of the ten top medical schools.

Step 2: Visualize yourself reaching those goals. The ability to do this is a major ingredient in success. A disproportionate number of highly successful people often visualize themselves succeeding. Before you go to bed tonight, imagine yourself reaching your goal (i.e., attending the Johns Hopkins Medical School or receiving a perfect report card).

Step 3: Eliminate any doubts about your ability to achieve your goals. Think positive. Keep saying aloud, "I can" and "I will." Action reinforces your belief in yourself.

Step 4: Don't let setbacks defeat you. Some of the greatest people in history succeeded only after facing many, many rejections. Remember, it's not how well you take victory but how well you take defeat.

Step 5: Hang around with students who have a strong internal locus of control. You'll learn from their example.

COLLEGE HEALTH SERVICES

Even with the best of self-care, preventive practices, and attitudes, students (especially freshmen) become sick. As a college student you won't have your mother around to take care of you. Your college's Health Services will have to suffice (provided you've paid the mandatory health care fee). The health facilities will be open twenty-four hours a day, seven days a week,.with registered nurses on duty and doctors on call at all times. If you're too sick to leave your dormitory room, have Health Services send an ambulance for you. Your doctor may admit you to the infirmary to recuperate.

You shouldn't visit Health Services only when you're deathly sick; your health plan will also provide psychological counseling, health education, diagnostic tests, X-rays, specialized consultations (i.e., dermatology, surgery, and ophthalmology), contraceptives, and prescriptions that can be filled at its pharmacy.

STRESS AND ANXIETY

Because everything and everybody is new and different at college, freshmen invariably find their first few months very stressful. In reaction to their new-found freedom and lifestyle, freshmen over-extend themselves in an effort to cram as many experiences as possible into their lives. Some common reasons for stress include a heavy work load, insufficient sleep, excessive extracurricular commitments, an unusually active social life, romantic and/or family difficulties, and poor grades.

Excessive stress can cause a wide range of psychological, emotional, and physical symptoms, including frequent migraines, changes in eating and sleeping habits, inability to concentrate, moodiness, irritability, heartbeat irregularities, alcohol and drug use, depression, apathy, teariness, fatigue, loneliness even when surrounded by friends, and inefficiency. If the stress isn't alleviated,

day-to-day activities can become overwhelming, and you'll break down both mentally and physically.

Since stress has such serious ramifications, you shouldn't ignore any of its symptoms. Your first step is to identify the sources of your stress and try to eliminate them. You should also try some of these suggestions:

• Get involved with outside activities. By volunteering to help others, you'll feel better about yourself and take your thoughts off your own troubles. Caution: volunteer if you have time, but don't overcommit.

• Exercise or do something physical. Physical activity often allows you to work off your mental stress. Besides, with the extra volume of blood rushing to your head, you may not even remember you have a problem, much less worry about it.

• Break your tasks into smaller, more manageable pieces so that you're not overwhelmed.

• Accept your limitations, and set realistic expectations for yourself. Forgive yourself for not being a superperson. Prioritize. Your health and schoolwork should occupy first and second place in your schema respectively. If you are stressed because you are short of time, drop some of your extracurricular activities. Allot your spare time wisely. During freshman year you should be seriously involved in only one or two activities. If even after cutting out all unnecessary time commitments you still feel anxious, drop all your extracurriculars or a course. Don't persist just to avoid being a quitter.

• Let some things go. When you can't do anything about a situation, stop stressing about it and go onto something else. Some things are just not worth your time, effort, and hassle. Don't stress about the little things; take care of the big ones and let the little problems resolve themselves.

• Practice visualization. Think of a relaxing, pleasant scene.

• Take time to relax, play, and sleep. You should take time every day to do something enjoyable and relaxing. Read a horror novel. Wear a new outfit. Shoot some baskets. Watch television. Listen to your favorite album. Go to a dance. Don't, however, let your good time stop you from studying or cut into your sleep time. Make sure to get at least seven hours of sleep everyday. If you become sleepy and have time, take a nap. Studies confirm that people who take naps tend to live longer.

• Seek help from your family, friends, clergy, teachers, deans, or peer advisors. Talking to them can give you a new perspective on or an alternative solution to your problem. It is better to talk about your stress than to let it fester inside you. If your problem seems very serious, seek professional assistance. You shouldn't be ashamed to visit your college's psychologist or psychiatrist. So many students need support once in a while that you'll probably have to wait for any appointment especially during midterm and finals weeks. Furthermore, your college counselor might be able to suggest some stress management workshops, cassettes, and books.

• Don't turn to artificial means, such as alcohol and drugs, for help and escape. You will only add to your problems.

• If the stress you encounter at college becomes unmanageable, don't hesitate to go home for a short vacation or take a semester off. Taking time off from college will give you a new perspective on your education and what it means to you. It will give you a chance to mature a bit more; you will be able to cope with college pressures more effectively once you decide to return. In the meantime, you may gain valuable work experience.

RELIGIONS AND CULTS

In times of stress and anxiety, many people find solace in religion. Your college will have places of worship and ministers for adherents of all the major world religions. Those students who attend religious services usually find the experience very comforting. When you feel depressed or anxious, you might want to talk to your minister. Since campus religious organizations often sponsor picnics, volunteer campaigns, get-togethers and Bible studies classes, you will also have the opportunity to meet other students with similar beliefs, attitudes, and upbringing.

Unfortunately, a large percentage of college age students neglect their religion. The number one reason cited for this is lack of time. Those students, however, who consider religion an important part of their life will find the necessary hour or two per week. During their college years, students frequently start to question their religious leanings; this is probably the real reason for lack of religious involvement among college-age people.

Since many college students don't have any religious affiliation, they tend to be easy recruits for cult groups like Sun Myung Moon's Unification Church or the People's Temple founded by Jim Jones. Since college is a very stressful time, many college students are lonely and depressed. There are more than 2,500 cult religions, which recruit thousands of high school and college students every year. Here's a rough idea of how cults recruit students:

Step 1: Cult members hang around psychological clinics in the hopes of finding students who are experiencing some type of turmoil that would make them especially weak and vulnerable. They also approach students who are eating in the cafeteria alone, thinking that these students might be so desperate for a group of friends that they become easy converts. Cult members often attempt to convert family and friends first. Most of those people who are recruited by cults are middle-class youths under twenty-five years of age.

Step 2: After singling you out, the cult member engages you in a friendly conversation in the hope of winning your trust. At the end of the conversation, the recruiter invites you to attend a dinner, to be followed by warm fellowship, songs, and discussions of life.

You are urged to participate actively in all these activities and to donate money to the cause.

Step 3: After the first dinner, you will be urged to sign up for longer retreats. Gradually you become more involved (i.e., you participate in fund-raising and disciplined rituals). In all likelihood, you won't even notice the gradual increase in your duties or the fact that your social life is beginning to revolve around the cult.

Step 4: Your ties to the outside world weaken and eventually disintegrate. Isolated from friends and family, you hear no counterarguments with which to refute the beliefs and practices of the group whose members punish those who disagree.

Step 5: You will be required to give 10 percent of your earnings to the group. This figure is soon upped to 25 percent; ultimately you will be ordered to give up all your money and possessions. The cult members give you ready excuses and counterarguments to use in case your family or friends question your motives, making you more resolute if your attitudes ever come into question.

Step 6: Threats of violence are used to stop members from leaving.

You're probably thinking that something like this could never happen to someone like you. Wrong. This is a very insidious process that can happen to anyone.

There are, however, ways to build resistance to persuasion. If you make a public commitment to your beliefs, you will be less susceptible to the beliefs of others. Having to defend your position actually makes you more committed to your beliefs and strengthens your resolve.

DIETING AND EXERCISE

Around midterms, you may start to see one effect of your college lifestyle accumulating around your waistline. This extra baggage is referred to as the "freshman fifteen." We know how this happens, but why? Before college, you probably depended on your parents to choose the types of foods served at mealtimes. Now that you are responsible for your own diet, you may be tempted to take shortcuts and gorge yourself on junk food. Further, to comfort themselves during periods of stress, freshmen sometimes turn to food. The major cause of freshman fifteen, however, is the cheap, filling food served all-you-can-eat-style in college meal halls.

Suppose one day you can't quite buckle your pants. Don't shove them in the back of your closet. Instead, keep them readily visible. Whenever you look at them, you'll strengthen your resolve to stay on your diet. The most important ingredient for a successful weight loss and maintenance program is willpower. Even if your resolve temporarily falters now and again, you will ultimately succeed.

Once you have the willpower, you need to find out the reasons for your overeating (e.g., boredom, depression) and condition yourself differently. If you're bored, go visit a friend or read a book—but don't eat.

FIRST DOWN, 15 TO GO

Below you'll find some dieting strategies to help you lose the freshman fifteen, or avoid gaining excess poundage in the first place:

- Regardless of your school's meal policy don't go off meal plan. Some schools permit freshmen to go off university food services, but with all the pressures of freshman year it will be too easy to miss meals and binge on junk food.

- Eat dinner with other students who are on a diet so that you can resist temptation even if tonight is Sunday Sundaes.

- Reduce your intake of salt, fat, and sugar, and add more protein to your diet. Stay away from fried and greasy foods such as hot dogs, hamburgers, french fries, and pastrami. Fortunately, most colleges have salad bars and broiled or boiled vegetarian entrees that provide low-calorie alternatives to the mystery meat entrees. Choose raw and cooked vegetables, fish, skinless chicken and turkey, fruits, and whole grains.

Warning: As a rule, I recommend you avoid cafeteria meats. In order to cut corners, college food contractors provide only fatty red meats. In addition, the meat is usually processed, meaning fat is mixed in with the meat, and unless you're a chemist you won't be able to separate the two components.

- College cafeterias (maybe in an effort to distract you from thinking about the main course) often offer a wide assortment of tempting and fattening desserts. Be careful about overindulging, because this is how you add those extra unwanted pounds. Some students eat only dessert when the main meal isn't to their liking. Not a good idea. You'll put on more weight faster by eating foods high in sugar.

Note: Often you will see these words in ingredients labels: fructose, sucrose, Nutrasweet, saccharin, and corn syrup. Don't be fooled— these are sugars or sugar substitutes.

- Don't use food to reward yourself. Whenever you accomplish something, read a good novel or watch a show on TV.

- Don't starve yourself. Some students are under the impression that all you have to do to lose weight is starve yourself for a few days, and presto! Problem solved. Unfortunately, weight lost in this manner consists mostly of water, which is readily replaced.

- Don't miss any meals. If you do, you'll probably overeat at the next meal.

- Chew your food slowly to avoid overeating just because your stomach hasn't had time to send a message to your brain that it's full.

- Don't go up for seconds; it's too tempting. Furthermore, you don't have to eat everything on your tray; you're not a garbage pail!

- Drink six or seven glasses of water every day. Studies conclude that drinking water helps you lose weight faster. Because the water fills and distends the stomach, it makes you feel full. Drink a glass of water right before dinner.

▪ Don't eat after 7 P.M., and never eat right before going to sleep. When you sleep you don't burn as many calories as when you're awake, so the food you just ate turns to fat. I find that when I brush my teeth right after dinner I don't snack afterwards because I'm too lazy to brush again. If you must snack at night, eat some of the low-calorie foods in your refrigerator.

▪ Limit your intake of beer and soft drinks. They contain many empty calories. Try drinking water, skim milk, or diluted fruit juices.

▪ Sometimes you get a craving for something sweet or salty. Take a nap or do something else and see if the urge goes away. If it doesn't and you crave something sugary, buy the chocolate bar but eat only half of it. Throw the remainder away.

▪ Get a small refrigerator and stock it with nutritious, low-calorie foods, such as celery sticks, carrots, rice cakes, unbuttered popcorn, apples, raw string beans, and green peppers.

Warning: Don't try any fad, quickie dieting techniques that promise to make you reduce at some phenomenal rate like ten pounds a week after the first week. Never use over-the-counter diet pills or diuretics. Liquid protein diets have been known to cause fatal arrythmias (irregular heart rhythms). People who have used them in the past have suffered from side effects ranging from tapeworm infections to death.

Even if you watch what you eat, you won't truly be in shape unless you exercise regularly. Exercising for a few hours each week (even a few hours of fast walking for a couple of hours per week) keeps your muscles toned and reduces your risk of certain diseases and ailments. Luckily, your college offers many types of fun physical activities so you needn't do some boring repetitive exercise routine over and over. You're sure to find some sport to your liking. Furthermore, most college activities are free or offered at a minimal charge.

If you still can't seem to manage your weight, your college's health services may have a nutritionist who can give you some more tips on losing weight and planning your exercise regimen in addition to analyzing your diet.

DRUGS AND ALCOHOL

Every college campus has students who drink and do drugs. At most parties, on and off campus, the drinks will be free of charge. On some campuses you will be able to find a party every night of the week, with plenty of beer and hard liquor, such as gin, vodka, and whiskey, available. These parties can sometimes get rough and wild, with fights occurring and students passing out from too much alcohol. Intoxicated people tend to do and say things they regret in the morning. Know your limits before you start drinking. Freshmen who have never been exposed to alcohol before should be very cautious at first; at every orientation there are one or two freshmen who drink to excess and end up sleeping in the school courtyard right where they passed out.

There are other risks besides those to your health. Since the legal drinking age in most states is twenty-one, most college students aren't able to drink legally yet. You risk being arrested by civil authorities, who aren't as lenient as campus police; a conviction, even a minor one, will haunt you for the rest of your life by barring you from certain graduate schools, jobs, and scholarships.

If, however, you do decide to drink, ask yourself why. Many students drink for the wrong reasons. Some use alcohol to feel more relaxed at social gatherings. Usually they end up acting foolish and then plead forgetfulness in the morning. Others drink because it makes them feel dangerous and wild. Still others do it to forget their problems, celebrate good times, or relieve stress and depression. A true alcoholic will drink for any reason. Alcohol is not a cure-all. It should be used only occasionally. When you start to use it consistently to get yourself through life's everyday problems, you need counseling. Your college provides services to help students with alcohol and other drug-related problems. Here are some important and lifesaving tips for those who drink:

• *Don't drive.* Since alcohol can impair your judgment and reasoning abilities, you or your friend might not realize that you've drunk too much to drive. If you've had more than one mixed drink, beer, or glass of wine in the past hour, you are probably legally drunk. Have a sober friend drive you, call a cab or the campus shuttle, or sleep over where you are. Moreover, don't allow an intoxicated friend to drive. Conveniently lose his car keys if he insists on driving.

Be especially careful when you drive during the weekends because approximately ten percent of those on the road are intoxicated.

▪ You and your friends should use the buddy system to protect one another. When you go drinking with your friends, look after one another. Be aware of the danger signs of overdosing. If your friend passes out but is arousable, turn him over on his stomach with his head turned to the side; this will prevent him from vomiting and suffocating. Watch him carefully for any signs that his condition is deteriorating. If he loses consciousness and doesn't respond to painful stimuli, then he has slipped into a coma. Call for medical help immediately.

▪ Don't drink on an empty stomach. Eat something before and during the party.

▪ Alternate drinking alcoholic beverages with nonalcoholic ones.

▪ Don't combine alcohol with any other drugs (medical or otherwise).

▪ Don't gulp or guzzle or chug down your drinks.

▪ Whenever possible, mix and pour your own drinks in order to control the amount of alcohol in each drink.

▪ Don't participate in drinking competitions.

▪ Drink only on weekends when you don't have to get up early the next morning for classes.

▪ If you lose count of the number of drinks you've had, STOP.

▪ If you are a woman, you should be aware that the negative effects of alcohol consumption are more pronounced in women. For example, women tend to become intoxicated quicker than men because women have a higher amount of body fat; a woman's body absorbs more alcohol during the time right before her menstrual period; and alcohol in large doses can reduce the effectiveness of some oral contraceptives and make the insertion of certain contraceptives difficult.

If you don't want to drink, don't feel that you have to. Although it is estimated that about ninety percent of college students drink once in a while, only about twenty-five percent of those students are considered problem drinkers. Therefore, it is possible to find a good percentage of students on every campus who drink moderately or abstain altogether. You'll feel most comfortable with friends who share values similar to your own. If, however, you are with a group of friends who drink, chances are good that they will feel uncomfortable and guilty with a nondrinker present, especially if you judge them or preach to them about the evils of imbibing. Respect their choice to drink. If they try to pressure you into drinking, politely ask them to respect your choice to abstain. You might, however, feel less conspicuous by nursing a beer throughout the evening or drinking a club soda; it will seem like you're sipping a gin and tonic.

Most people believe that after a few drinks they become more sociable and witty. Some students even fancy themselves the life of the party. Usually they become the spectacle of the party with their ludicrous antics. One of the casualties of drinking is good communication; students who are intoxicated tend to talk more, listen less, and interrupt others while speaking. Here are some other ways alcohol wreaks havoc on relationships:

▪ When under the influence of alcohol, students tend to have more sexual encounters than they would normally.

▪ Since students under the effects of alcohol don't worry about pregnancy or sexually transmitted diseases such as AIDS, their sexual encounters often turn into sexual misadventures. As a direct result of their intoxication, many students forget to use contraceptives, and those who do remember often use the contraceptive incorrectly.

▪ Sexual assault occurs more frequently when one or both people are intoxicated. In all reported cases of gang rape alcohol consumption has played a pivotal role. Under certain states' laws, it is rape if a person has sex with another person who is legally intoxicated. Intoxication isn't an excuse for forcing sex with another person.

▪ Alcohol causes sexual dysfunction in both men and women. Men fail to have erections and women have more difficulty achieving orgasm. Excessive drinking on a continuous basis also causes testicular atrophy, impotence, and breast enlargement in men.

SAFE SEX

If you decide to have sex during your college career, you'll need to take certain precautions. You will have to guard against not only unwanted pregnancy but also sexually transmitted diseases. You and your partner should talk about prevention before having sex. Even though this might make one or both of you uncomfortable, you don't want to take unnecessary chances with your and your partner's health.

There are many types of birth control devices on the market. You will probably be able to get many of them through your college's health services. Students don't realize that although contraceptives such as the pill and diaphragm prevent unwanted pregnancy, they don't prevent the transmission of sexually transmitted diseases (STDs). You must take this matter seriously, because STDs can be the cause of major health problems. For instance, gonorrhea can cause sterility; the tertiary stage of syphilis can cause blindness, paralysis, and mental disturbances; herpes can cause cancer of the cervix; and AIDS is always fatal.

Latex condoms used in conjunction with a vaginal spermicide offer the best protection against STDs and vaginal infections. The condom is very effective in providing protection from unwanted pregnancy, gonorrhea, trichomoniasis, syphilis, AIDS and, to a lesser extent, herpes and genital warts. Although condoms cause no harmful side effects, very often people refuse to use them; students call them nasty rubbers and claim they spoil the mood or don't feel good. No birth control or disease-prevention method, however, is without side effects. Even if your partner swears that he or she has no sexually transmitted disease, you should still use a condom; very often sexually transmitted diseases are asymptomatic. Moreover, surveys show that in order to have sex, an alarming number of people lie about the number of previous partners and sexual encounters they've had. Decide for yourself whether to act responsibly.

Condoms can be purchased at any drugstore without a prescription. They are inexpensive (your college's health services may even give them to students free of charge) and disposable. When used properly and with a spermicidal cream or foam (i.e., non-oxynol-9), the condom is a very effective form of birth control. Store your condoms in a cool place and replace them if they're not used after two years (there will be an expiration date on the package) because the rubber weakens and eventually deteriorates with heat and age. In addition, you shouldn't be excessively rough with them because they can tear. Take special pains to make sure you and your partner have the best protection possible.

HOW SAFE IS YOUR COLLEGE CAMPUS?

Because many colleges are located in idyllic settings, students and their parents are often under the erroneous impression that the campus is a haven from the ills of society. Just because your college is in the middle of cow country or on the outskirts of a quaint New England town complete with cobblestone streets, DON'T BE MIS-LED!!! College campuses are plagued by the same social problems as society at large. Robbery, assault, rape, and even murder occur at colleges around the nation. Some studies have concluded that certain crimes, such as rapes and burglaries, occur even more frequently on college campuses than they do in many cities. Since most people are so busy looking for suspicious-looking people, they fail to realize that most campus crimes (approximately 85 percent) are committed by students and their friends and dates. At some college campuses, security problems are made even worse because students fail to take adequate safety precautions. Before you arrive at school, assess how safe the campus is by asking questions such as:

- Is the campus situated in a high crime area?
- Does your college have an escort and/or shuttle service and student patrols?
- Are there emergency telephones strategically placed around the campus?
- How well lit are the campus and parking lots? Are there many dark areas full of bushes and shrubs? Are the parking areas close

to the dormitories? Most assaults, burglaries, and violent crimes are committed at night.

- How many security officers are there per student?
- How secure are doors and windows? How well are the doors and windows constructed?
- Does your dormitory building have many unlocked dark storage rooms in the basement or attic?

CAMPUS SAFETY TIPS

If your college needs to take additional safety measures, you should talk to the school's officials. There are also certain precautions you can take to increase your personal safety.

In the dormitory:

- When you first arrive at your school, change the lock on your door. The student(s) who had your room last year might have made a duplicate key for your room.

- Don't leave the dorm building door or your room door unlocked or open even when you're in your room. Because students are too lazy to take out their keys they prop open doors. Anybody can just walk into the building and into an unsuspecting student's room. Believe it or not, a substantial number of students leave their doors unlocked and even ajar when they go to sleep at night. Promise me you'll never do this.

- Don't open the door unless you know who is knocking.

- Try not to keep valuables (e.g., large amounts of money or expensive jewelry) in your dormitory room.

- Report broken windows, doors, and locks to the college's residential life office.

- Be careful about bringing acquaintances to your room; in the majority of sexual assault cases the woman knows her attacker.

- Report suspicious persons in or lurking around the dormitory to campus security.

• Engrave your portable valuables with your name and social security number. Your campus security office will probably be able to loan you an engraver. In case they are stolen and the police recover your possessions, you will be able to readily identify them.

When you leave:

• Don't leave your bicycle outside. Chain it to the radiator in your room.

• Your computer and stereo equipment should be locked away in your closet or in a high-security lock-up if you can't take them with you when you leave for vacation. Computers, stereos, cameras, and other portable valuables are often stolen on college campuses. Take the necessary precautions.

• Never leave or lend your keys to a friend. Your key could be lost and duplicated. If you need your plants watered or your fish fed while you're away, move them to your friend's room.

Out and about campus:

• Don't carry your keys and identification together on the same key ring or in the same purse or pocket.

• Avoid desolate areas (i.e., laboratories and library stacks and sublevels at night).

• Try not to walk or jog alone at night. If you have to go somewhere, bring a friend or two or take the shuttle. If it's midnight, you're leaving the library alone, and the shuttle bus isn't running because it's Sunday, wait in the lobby of the library until you see a group of students heading in the general direction of your destination. Then follow the group at a close distance.

• Know where the emergency telephones are located.

• Remain alert when walking. This doesn't mean you have to constantly look behind you or cast furtive glances all about. It does mean that you should be aware of your surroundings at all times; don't daydream. Moreover, evil-intentioned people will be less likely to bother with you if you walk like you have a purpose, as evidenced by your sure, confident strides. Duck into a store or other busy public place and ask the proprietor to call the police if you suspect someone is following you.

- Don't scream "Help" if you're being attacked; scream "Fire." People might not want to get involved if they think that you're being mugged or raped but they are often eager to watch a fire.

- Walk only in well-lit areas that are frequented by your friends and classmates. Don't take a shortcut in order to save time.

- Whenever you go somewhere, especially at night, make sure you have enough money for a taxi or a bus. Never hitchhike!

- Have your keys ready before you reach the door so that you won't have to stand around fumbling for them.

- Don't carry much cash or any valuable jewelry. Turn your rings around so the stones aren't visible. Pull your sleeves down and pull up your collar to conceal any bracelets or necklaces you're wearing.

- Try not to use the automatic teller machines at night. Many, many people are mugged while getting cash. Furthermore, don't write down your access number; memorize it or, if you must, write it in your address and telephone book disguised as a telephone number.

- Be careful if you carry mace, key rings with sharpened points, and other types of weapons for protection. There have been cases where the attacker has wrested the weapon away from and used it on his target.

Travel by bicycle:

- Have your bicycle registered with the campus police and security. They will engrave your identification number on your bicycle. You will then be given a sticker to put on your bicycle to alert would-be thieves that your bicycle is engraved and registered with the local law enforcement agency. Your bicycle won't be stolen so quickly because the engraved I.D. number will lower its resale value.

- Never leave your bicycle on the street unattended, even for a moment. Park it in a well-lit area.

- Don't leave your locked bicycle on the street for long.

- If you don't take your bike home with you during vacation, chain it to the radiator in your room. This will make a thief's job harder by degrees.

Travel by car:

- Try to avoid walking alone in parking lots at night.

- Have your keys in your hands as you near your vehicle.

- Check the back seats before you open the car door.

- Lock the doors once you get into the car.

- Keep your car in good condition to minimize your chances of getting stranded somewhere. You should always make sure that you have enough gas to get home or to the nearest gasoline station.

- If you find yourself stranded in a unfamiliar area, put up the hood or attach a white cloth to your antenna and remain locked in the car. If someone other than a police officer stops, don't open your locked door; ask the person to call the police.

- Park your car in a well-lit busy area close to your dormitory.

- Never leave any valuables in full view. Hide your purse, camera, and tape recorder in the trunk, not the glove compartment (that's the first place thieves look).

- Always lock your car when you leave, even if it's only for a second.

- Lock the doors and close the windows of your car when you drive through high-crime neighborhoods.

- Regardless of the circumstances, never pick up hitchhikers.

Even if you are super cautious, you may find yourself the victim of an assault, in which case you should do the following:

- Remain calm and try to assess your options. Can you run, escape, scream, fight back, or somehow attract attention to your plight?

- Take note of the attacker's appearance. Try to remember exactly what he said.

- If you are threatened with or the victim of an assault or robbery, notify the police immediately.

SEXUAL ASSAULT

As odd as it seems, many men and even women do not know what constitutes a legal rape. Studies of college males who were asked if they ever forced sex show a surprising number of men answering in the affirmative. Even more surprising, these men did not consider themselves rapists. They did not realize that they could have been convicted of a criminal offense. Women often report that a date rapist asked to see them again, as if no crime had happened. Thus, it's important to dispel some myths concerning date and stranger rape.

Myth 1: Although college campuses have their share of rapes and sexual assaults, their incidence is much lower than for society at large. Many students and their parents don't realize how prevalent campus rape is. Contrary to common opinion, college campuses have a higher incidence of rape than some major cities in the United States. Studies estimate that about one in four college women will be the victim of a rape or attempted rape; more than half of all college coeds personally know a rape victim. As a subgroup, freshmen have the highest incidence of rape. The first three weeks of freshman year are when rapes occur most frequently.

Myth 2: Rape is not premeditated. Some rapes are premeditated. A number of rapists report stalking their victims for days. Others hide in dark alleys waiting for a victim to happen along.

Myth 3: Rapists fit a certain profile. Most people picture a rapist as a slimy mutant jumping out of the sewers and raping his victim at knifepoint behind the cover of bushes. Although some rapes do occur this way, most do not. Often the assailant is someone the woman trusted and knew—maybe a friend, a date, or a dorm mate. Stranger rapes are committed by ordinary looking people. You have to be on the lookout for mutants in sheep skins. According to recent research, the most likely rapists are male friends who are sexually aggressive.

Warning: Some statistics conclude that one out of three date rapes on campus is committed by an athlete. Some schools even have mandatory rape prevention workshops for their student athletes. Fraternity members also commit a high percentage of campus rapes.

Myth 4: Even though the woman doesn't give her consent, it is not considered rape if she doesn't fight back. Any time a male uses actual or implied force to have sex with a woman, the act constitutes rape. Many women are too overpowered, frightened, and intimidated to struggle physically. Acquaintance or date rapists usually use threats and bodily strength instead of weapons to force the woman to submit.

Myth 5: Rapists are motivated by a desire for sex. Along with a desire for sexual gratification, many rapists rape in order to feel powerful and dominant.

Myth 6: Rapists carefully choose their victims. Women often think that if they dress conservatively and look plain they will be safer. However, rapists usually just choose the next woman who walks by.

Myth 7: "It can't happen to me." No matter what type of precautions you take, you can still be the victim of a sexual assault.

Myth 8: Women cry rape. This rarely occurs in light of the difficulties in reporting and prosecuting a rape.

The seriousness of date rape cannot be overemphasized. Survivors of date rape often find it impossible to have a normal relationship for a long time afterwards. Women who were raped by a stranger have panic attacks if left alone and are afraid to venture outdoors after dark. Many survivors of college rape find the experience so traumatic they leave school.

Below are several steps you can take to protect yourself against date rape.

- Attend a self-defense class. It will help you learn and practice strategies for reacting to an assault.

- Imagine some assault scenarios. Role-play your responses alone or with friends, and try to evaluate them. This can help you improve your response time in case you ever are assaulted.

- Be careful about whom you choose as friends and dates. Try to choose students who have values and priorities similar to your own. When you hang around people with more permissive sexual attitudes, others will believe that you too share these same values.

- Keep your date public. Go to public places that are frequented by many others. Have money so that you can get home by yourself in case you find yourself feeling uncomfortable with your date. If possible, go on group dates in the beginning until you know the person better.

- Consider the messages you might be sending. Certain behaviors, such as dressing provocatively and flirting, are interpreted as an invitation to a sexual encounter. Be alert to the types of ideas your actions are generating, and make your intentions perfectly clear.

- You don't owe your date anything because he spent money on you. Some men believe that their dates owe them sex or some "feels" in return for paying for the dinner and entertainment. Just remember, your body is not for sale.

- Drugs and alcohol are usually associated with date rape because they affect your judgment. If you decide to drink, do it responsibly.

- Be careful at fraternity parties. The majority of gang rapes occur at frat parties; a good percentage of these rapes are committed by student athletes. Gang rapes have also been used as fraternity initiation rituals. Even seemingly upright and moral students participate in gang rapes; people act differently when in a group, which deindividualizes the members and makes each member feel anonymous and thus unaccountable for the crime. Gang rape is a heinous crime for which each and every participant can be severely punished.

▪ Beware of a relationship that is progressing along the lines of the passive female/dominant male stereotype. For example, does he insist on paying for everything all the time? Does he make all the decisions on the date? This should be a warning sign to you that you might be falling into a dependent role.

▪ Think twice before you go to a man's room or invite him to yours; these are the places where most rapes occur.

▪ Decide in advance how far you intend to go. For instance, you might want to say, "I would like to hold hands and kiss a bit tonight. I, however, definitely don't intend to go any further." If he goes past your sexual limit, firmly yet tactfully stop him. If he continues, be very LOUD in voicing your disapproval. The most effective response seems to be, "You are raping me. I'm calling the police." If you don't speak up you will be reinforcing the notion that "no" means "yes." Don't let him bully, pressure, or guilt you into going any further. Nobody has the right to demand sexual activity from anybody.

▪ A woman should fight back physically if she can because 1) it will be easier to prosecute her case if there are clear signs of resistance, b) two studies have found no evidence that resistance influences the likelihood of injury, and c) women who resist their attacker experience less post-rape trauma.

▪ Respect your date's right to refuse any type of sexual activity.

A woman who is raped should get help immediately from relatives and close friends. She shouldn't be alone. She should also call the police and report the crime even if she doesn't intend to press formal charges. By reporting the rape she may save another woman from a similar fate; date and stranger rapists are often repeat offenders. She should seek medical and psychological assistance to minimize the physical and psychological aftereffects of the attack.

Colleges provide continuing counseling to help women through the experience so that they bear as few scars as possible.

EXHIBITIONISM

Flashers get turned on by showing their private parts to strangers. They derive pleasure from scaring their victim. If you've been flashed, don't show any reaction because exhibitionists become sexually excited by seeing fear or disgust reflected on your face. Get away as quickly as possible; in some instances flashing has served as a prelude to sexual assault. When you are a safe distance away, report the incident to the police.

SEXUAL HARASSMENT

Sexual harassment is the use of one's authority to force sexual activity with another person. At college, sexual harassment cases usually involve a male professor and one of his female students. Cases of homosexual harassment have also been reported.

If you find yourself the victim of sexual harassment, you should: 1) tactfully let the harasser know you don't appreciate his/her advances; 2) talk to the college's Dean of Student Life about your problem; she can help you make a formal complaint; and 3) change or drop the class if the harassment continues.

OBSCENE PHONE CALLS

While at college you might receive an obscene or prank call that will start with the caller describing his sexual exploits or threatening you with statements such as, "I've been following you" or "I'm coming for you." The caller may pose as a sex researcher who is conducting a survey on women's bathing habits, lingerie, or contraceptives.

Here are some tips for preventing and dealing with obscene phone calls:

• Never mention your name or number on an answering machine message. You don't want to give callers any information at all about yourself. Record something like, "Hi, I can't come to the phone right now but if you leave a message after the beep I'll get back to you as soon as possible." According to studies, the majority of obscene callers are male and their victims are women. Thus, women might want to lower their voices when recording a machine message.

• When someone calls your number by mistake, just say, "Sorry, wrong number." Don't volunteer your number.

• Don't let the caller know you are home alone.

• If you do hear an improper question or an obscenity, stay calm and hang up *immediately*. Since the goal of the caller is to get a shocked or disgusted reaction from you, don't slam the phone down on the receiver.

• If the obscene phone calls continue, report them to campus security or the telephone company so that a tracer can be hooked up to your phone. Since obscene phone calls are illegal, the caller risks punishment by campus and civil authorities if caught. You should also change your phone number to an unlisted one or list only your first initial and last name in the phone book.

• Since a large number of obscene and prank calls are made by acquaintances, you should tell only your closest friends, family members, and the campus security.

12

Money
Matters

Every year colleges raise their tuition to keep up with inflation, and as a result most students and their parents are left trying to scrape together enough money for a college education. Many a college career has been started and then abruptly terminated by financial difficulties. Since few students are immune to financial worries, this chapter can prove extremely helpful.

FINANCIAL AID

On some college campuses, more than fifty percent of students receive some type of financial aid from the school and/or the federal government. Although this number might seem large, it still leaves many financially qualified students without sufficient aid. Why? There are a number of reasons, but the most common ones are that 1) the many forms are very confusing and complicated, 2) the student and his or her parents don't realize they qualify, or 3) the student is too embarrassed to apply for financial aid. None of these reasons is valid.

Each year students are required to fill out all kinds of financial aid forms by a certain deadline. Be prompt! If you are late, available funds might already be allocated; aid is often given out on a first-come-first-served basis. The forms are deliberately made long and frustrating to discourage all but the most determined. You should, however, make filling out these forms your number one priority. The few hours that you spend completing them may alleviate many of your financial problems and allow you to continue your education. If you have trouble with some questions, talk to a financial aid officer at your school.

Most loans and grants from colleges and the federal government are available only on a need basis. Your college financial aid officers will make up an expense budget, including among other things the cost of room, board, tuition, books, and traveling. Then the family's contribution will be calculated, taking into account the assets, expenses, savings, and earnings of both you and your parents. The difference between the projected year's expenses and the family's estimated contribution is considered your financial need. If eligible for financial help, you will receive an aid package consisting of a combination of grants, loans, and work study. Grants are essentially free money; they don't have to be repaid. Government loans are also desirable because of their very low interest rates and deferred interest payments. Work study, which will be discussed further in the section on term-time employment, allows a student to work at an on-campus job during the school term to earn money for college. Your college will help place you in a job in one of the various college offices, gymnasiums, laboratories, cafeterias, dormitories, or libraries. Because the jobs require only unskilled labor, the pay is often minimal. Often students work ten to fifteen hours a week because they are limited in how much they can earn in any one term.

Since college costs rise each year, the amount of available financial aid must also increase to keep college affordable. In these rapidly changing times, too many students and parents don't realize that they might be eligible for financial aid. You owe it to yourself to thoroughly investigate all the possibilities.

If you've been given a financial aid package that doesn't adequately cover your projected expenses, your first recourse is to visit the financial aid office at your college. Tell the financial aid officer your problem; since your aid package isn't inscribed in stone, there may be some way to make the combination of grants, loans, and work study more attractive.

If you're still short of money, don't worry yet. There are plenty of private scholarships sponsored by unions, religious organizations, civic groups, and local clubs for which you can apply. Many of these scholarships don't require any proof of financial need. You'll qualify for some of them if you or your parent is a veteran, military officer, fraternity member, union worker, employee of a participating company, or member of a certain ethnic, racial, religious, or political group. If you are eligible, you'll need a good average and some significant extracurricular commitments to have a chance of winning the scholarship. For a fee, some organizations will run computerized scholarship searches for students, but with a little research you can do the same thing. There are plenty of books in your local library with detailed listings of various types of available scholarships.

Note: If you are on financial aid and you win an outside scholarship, your college will take a percentage (sometimes as much as fifty percent) of the money to reduce the amount of grant money you receive from the college. If you or your scholarship sponsor report the outside scholarship to your college, be prepared to share the booty.

Sometimes, students and parents, although they're eligible for financial aid, don't ask for it because they are too embarrassed. In this case, as in many others, pride has a high sticker price. Just keep in mind that it is your tax money that pays for the financial aid programs. Take advantage of the opportunity; it might be the crucial factor that allows you to continue your education.

EMPLOYMENT

Many college students hold jobs during the school year and during the summer. Some students take a job for the money, others for the on-job experience and skills they can acquire, and still others for the impression certain jobs make on a resume. If you are seeking a job that requires only unskilled labor, you will have no problem finding one, because such jobs are plentiful. This section, however, is designed to help you to find and get the more competitive jobs.

TERM-TIME EMPLOYMENT

If you are thinking of taking a part-time job, you should consider how many hours you can work so that your grades won't suffer, what types of jobs are available, what kind of job you should look for, how to find and get the job, and what kind of help is available to you in locating it.

Since school is a student's primary concern, most can work only ten to fifteen hours per week during the school year. Studies have shown that this time commitment doesn't negatively affect a student's grade point average. Don't, however, work more than twenty hours per week because then your grades will probably falter.

Since you'll be able to work only a few hours per day, you won't have many jobs from which to choose. Most students find employment on-campus because the work schedules for these jobs are extremely flexible. Working on campus can sometimes be loads of fun, especially if your work involves meeting other students. On the flip side, most campus jobs pay minimum wage and require no skills. How do you feel about working in the basement of the cafeteria cleaning off your classmates' dinner trays? Doesn't sound too pleasant, yet cafeteria work is what many students end up doing, because the jobs are plentiful and easy to get. I consider cafeteria work a major waste of time. If you need the money, you would be better off taking out a student loan, saving every penny you make during the summer, or cutting corners closely during the year; spend your extra free time increasing your G.P.A. and getting involved in a few meaningful extracurricular activities.

Working can cause its share of problems. As a freshman, Jason found on-campus work as a janitor cleaning dormitory lounges and halls for minimum wage. Since the work was especially taxing, he never had enough energy or time to get involved with extracurricular activities. Although capable of a sterling grade point average (he was valedictorian of his high school class) his job commitment prevented him from dedicating himself to his course work. For four years he worked at the same job. During his senior year he decided to apply to law school. With his mediocre average, unimpressive janitorial job, and insignificant extracurricular involvement, Jason was accepted only at a law school with a very poor academic reputation. You'll have to decide if you want the immediate cash at

the expense of your academics, extracurriculars, friends, and future.

If you do decide that you must work, you won't have to settle for a menial, low-paying job if you expend some effort. Start looking early in the term because if you wait, many of the best positions will already be taken. Your first step is to assess your strongest points. Ask yourself, "What qualities, traits, skills, knowledge, and/or experiences do I have that would make someone want to hire me?" Your next step is to visit your college's career placement office and meet with a placement officer who can give you some idea of what types of jobs are available and how to write your resume and cover letter to capitalize on your assets. The placement center will also have a binder and/or a bulletin board full of job listings, with the job's description, rate of pay, requirements, and the employer's name and number.

Your professors, parents, relatives, family doctor, friends and their parents can also help you find a job. If you have been referred by someone, make sure to use his or her name when you go on an interview or send a cover letter. Employers will be more eager to hire those applicants who come highly recommended by someone they respect.

As you consider prospective jobs, answer these questions:

- How much money do you want to work for? How much money do you need? Money should not be your sole consideration in selecting employment. Off-campus jobs usually pay more but aren't as convenient as on-campus jobs in terms of schedule and location. You might consider taking a job that has lower wages but has other perks.

- What type of time commitment does the job entail? Can you make your own hours and/or work at home? Will it interfere with your other commitments? Never miss class because of your job. Schoolwork takes first priority. You might be able to schedule your sections and study groups around your work schedule, but don't choose classes because of your job's time commitment.

- Is the job easy or difficult, physical or mental, fun or boring?

- What qualifications do you need (e.g., typing, shorthand, laboratory experience)? You will have a wider selection of employment choices if you possess such skills.

- What types of fringe benefits accompany the job? For instance, those who work in department stores usually receive discounts on store merchandise. Investigate any fringe benefits the job might have before deciding not to consider it.

- Will this job teach you any new skills or utilize those you already have?

- Will this job add to your resume when you apply for graduate schools or employment in your senior year? A student who wants to be a physicist would benefit from taking a job as a research assistant in a physics laboratory, rather than working at a pizza delivery job.

Once you've devised a list of acceptable employment prospects, it's time for you to make some phone calls and visits. When you call, ask to speak to a specific person. Inquire about the job opening. If the employer wants to see you in person, bring your resume along with you. Further on in this chapter we offer some tips for your resume, cover letter, and interview. After you've sent out resumes and been interviewed, make some follow-up calls or visits.

SUMMER EMPLOYMENT

Unlike term-time employment, summer employment is a must. Graduate school admissions officers, scholarship committees, and post-graduate school employers will want to know how you spent your undergraduate summers. Tanning or loafing won't strengthen your future applications. In addition, summer jobs tend to be more prestigious than term-time jobs. Thus, you need to concentrate on finding a job that will look good on your resume and help you in your studies or prospective career. Unfortunately, some of the country's most prestigious jobs are unpaid. Don't shy away from unpaid internships; in the future, the experience might prove to be priceless.

The procedure for securing summer employment is similar to that for term-time employment with only one or two additional sidenotes. For instance, you will have to start your search for a summer job much earlier than you would have for a semester job. Employers begin to conduct information seminars and on-campus interviews as early as October for summer positions starting in May. Don't wait until after the January break to look.

In addition, when you visit the career center remember to ask for the summer employment notebook. This volume is filled with upperclassmen's summer employment questionnaires with answers to questions such as: What did you learn from the job? Was it a worthwhile experience and would you recommend it to others? What was your rate of payment? Would the employer be willing to hire more students from your school? If so, how and who should students contact? This file may give you some good leads.

COVER LETTERS AND RESUMES

In this section are some pointers for writing cover letters and resumes, both of which are vital to your employment prospects. Remember, they are your introduction to your prospective employers.

Tips For Cover Letter

• Address the cover letter to a specific person. Never send it to "Whomever It May Concern" or "Director of Recruitment."

• Specifically target your cover letter for the company you are applying for. Include information about the organization as it pertains to you.

• Be sure to explain who you are and why you are writing in your opening paragraph.

• Use the middle paragraph to sell yourself.

• In the last paragraph tell the employer how and when you will be in touch with them. Don't leave it up to the employer to get in touch with you.

• Center the writing in the middle of the page.

• Don't let the cover letter or the resume exceed one page.

Tips for Your Resume

• Place your full name in bold type at the top of the page.

• Don't include an objective. Students usually make their objective too vague, and many employment recruiters use it to weed out applicants.

• Never include your height, marital situation, weight, age, health, religion, political leanings, or ethnic background.

P.O. Box 3487
Brown University
Providence, RI 02912
(401) 865-1223
January 31, 1989

Mr. William Rivers
Director, Human Resources
Foreign Policy Magazine
312 Rhubarb Road
Providence, Rhode Island 02917

Dear Mr. Rivers,

My independent study advisor, Professor John Smythe, suggested I write to
you about internship opportunities with *Foreign Policy* magazine. I am a
sophomore at Brown University, double majoring in Political Science and
Modern European History and I am very interested in a career in foreign
policy and international law.

With my writing/research experience and commitment in foreign affairs, I
believe I would be a valuable asset to your summer internship program. I
am currently the co-chairperson for the International Relations Department
Undergraduate Group and I am also a staff writer for the *Brown Foreign
Affairs Journal*. In addition, I am doing an independent study project on
Soviet economic reforms this semester.

Enclosed you will find my resume and copies of a few of my published
articles on Russia, Eastern Europe and the Middle East. I will contact you in
the near future to ascertain whether you received my materials and
hopefully to set up an appointment to further discuss internship
opportunities with *Foreign Policy*. Thank you very much for your
consideration.

Sincerely,

Terry R. Smith

CHRONOLOGICAL RÉSUMÉ

Terry R. Smith

P.O. Box 3487   89-34 125 Street
Brown University   Cambridge, Massachusetts 43001
Providence, Rhode Island 02912   (709) 451-6878
(401) 865-1223

Education
    Brown University, Providence, RI. (1987-present)
       • Majors: Anticipate Honors B.A. in Political Science, B.A. in Modern European
       History
       • 3.83 cumulative GPA
    Potter Park High School, Cambridge, MA (1983-87)
       • Valedictorian in class of 552; 4.0 GPA

Previous Employment
    Legal Intern, Carlton, Brown and Brazelton, New York, New York (Summer '88)
       • Researched and wrote legal briefs and entries
       • Liaison for attorneys, police officials, witnesses, judges and other court officials
       • Attended bi-weekly seminars given by distinguished legal figures
    Legal Intern, Christiansen, Wilson, Pratt and Oliver, Cambridge, MA (Summer '87)
       • Researched information for discrimination cases
       • Presented data at settlement meetings
       • Served legal documents
       • Updated law library and indexed and organized documents
    Counselor, East Coast Experience, Andover, MA (Summer '86)
       • Taught advanced level computer languages to campers age 10-16 years of age
       • Acted as senior residential counselor to 15 teenagers
       • Planned and designed special activities for entire camp

Extracurricular Activities
    Secretary, Brown Debate Union (1987-present)
       • Organized and scheduled debate tournaments
    Co-chairperson, International Relations Department Undergraduate Group (1987-
    present)
       • Oversaw day-to-day operations of student advising network
       • Assisted in the publication of the *International Relations Faculty Yellow Pages*
    Staff Writer and Copy Editor, Brown Foreign Affairs Journal (1987-present)
       • Researched and wrote articles on the U.S.S.R. and the Middle East
    President, Potter Park High School Parliamentary Debate Team (1986-87)
       • Revitalized failing team; membership rose from 20 to over 100
    Chairperson/Organizer, Potter Park High's "Career Forums" (1985)
       • Recruited guest speakers to come and address the senior classes on career issues
       • Ran weekly meetings to plan and schedule events

Awards and Achievements
    Potter Park Alumni Award
    National Merit Scholarship finalist
    Lincoln Hays Memorial Award and Scholarship
    State Champion, Debate 1985, 1986, 1987
    State Champion, Massachusetts Mock Trial 1986

Other Skills and Interests
    Languages: Fluent in French and Spanish; beginning Russian
    Computer Literacy: Working knowledge of Microsoft Word, Word Perfect and Excel

SKILLS RÉSUMÉ

Terry R. Smith

P.O. Box 3487
Brown University
Providence, Rhode Island 02912
(401) 454-1212

89-34 125 Street
Cambridge, Massachusetts 43001
(709) 451-6878

Education
Brown University, Providence, RI. (1987-present)
  • Majors: Honors B.A. in Political Science, B.A. in Modern European History
  • Senior Honors Thesis on Legal Aspects of Soviet Economic Reform
  • Elected junior year to Phi Beta Kappa; 3.9 cumulative GPA
Potter Park High School, Cambridge, Massachusetts. (1983-87)
  • Valedictorian in class of 552; 4.0 GPA

Writing/Research Experience
Research Assistant-Soviet Foreign Economics Project, Center for Foreign Policy
  Development, Providence, RI. (Summer '90)
  • Assisted in maintaining a database on Soviet-Western Joint Ventures
  • Designed marketing strategy for database
  • Research on Europe, the Persian Gulf, and U.S.-Soviet relations
  • Helped in administration of international conferences
Editor, Brown Foreign Affairs Journal, Providence, RI (1988-present)
  • Solicited, choose and edited articles
  • Managed a staff of about 30 regarding all aspects of the journal's production
Editorial Assistant, Foreign Policy magazine, Providence, RI (Summer 1989)
  • Researched, fact-checked, and edited manuscripts
Chairperson, International Relations Department Undergraduate Group (1988-
  present)
  • Planned lectures, organized meetings, published the *International Relations
  Faculty Yellow Pages*
Legal Intern, Carlton, Brown and Brazelton, Cambridge, MA (Summer 1988)
  • Researched and wrote legal briefs and entries
  • Recorded depositions, conducted interviews, served subpoenas, collected
  evidence and testified in court
Legal Intern, Christiansen, Wilson, Pratt and Oliver, Cambridge, MA (Summer '87)

Communications/Interpersonal Skills
President, Brown Debate Union (1989-present)
  • Presided over meetings of more than 100 debaters and judges
  • Implemented a freshman recruiting and training program which resulted in a
  200% increase in tournament attendance
Co-president, Brown Debate Union (1989)
  • Started a program whereby Brown debaters coach local high school teams

Relevant Awards and Achievements
The United States Congressional Harry S. Truman Scholarship in Government
  (Massachusetts State Winner)
Ratcliffe T. Hicks Prize for Excellence in Debating Award
Brown representative, World Debate Championships in Scotland
Top ranked judge, American Parliamentary Debate tournaments
State Champion, Debate 1985, 1986, 1987
State Champion, Massachusetts Mock Trial 1986

Other Skills and Interests
*Languages:*Fluent in French and Spanish; beginning Russian
*Computer Literacy:*Working knowledge of Microsoft Word, Word Perfect, Excel, Lotus
  123 and PFS Write

- Place your permanent and current phone numbers and addresses in the upper right and left corners.

- List your academic background and degrees in reverse chronological order.

- Include your grade point average only if it is exceptional (i.e., 3.5 or better).

- Be concise. Don't pad your resume with incidentals.

- Freshmen and sophomores may include their high school awards, honors, employment, and extracurriculars.

- Be sure to stress your strongest points on your resume. Don't go into great detail about your waitress job and give only a passing sentence to your editorial position on the campus daily newspaper. In order to emphasize something even more, you might want to break the reverse chronological order; for instance, even though your waitress job is more recent than your editorial job, you might want to list your editorial position first.

- Depending on your focus, you might want to highlight either your job title or where you worked.

- Use only powerful active verbs (e.g., analyzed, formulated, designed, assessed) to describe your extracurricular activities and employment responsibilities. Passive verbs (such as "was improved" or "was supervised") weigh prose down and make it (and you) seem listless. Omit superfluous words such as "responsibilities include."

- Since college students don't have years of employment experience, place the dates of your employment and service on the right hand side of the page. This deemphasizes them.

- Try to keep at least an inch border around the text.

- Never send out a photocopy of your resume. Get copies of it professionally printed on good quality paper (i.e., paper with a linen or cotton content) with matching envelopes. Don't use white paper. Use off-white, gray, beige or tan to give your resume, cover letter, and envelopes a professional look.

▪ You don't need to end your resume with "References available upon request." The employers knows that you will have references ready in case you are asked for them.

In this section you will find two sample resumes and a sample cover letter. The first is the basic chronological resume, and the second is a skills resume. The chronological resume should be used when the position requires no specific skills or when you don't know what skills are needed. The chronological resume is usually used by freshmen and sophomores because their course of study, extracurricular achievements, and work experience are not focused enough to fill a skills resume. The skills resume is a much stronger resume because it focuses on the positions the applicant has held and the specific skills needed for the job.

HOW TO MAKE A GOOD IMPRESSION DURING AN INTERVIEW

There are a number of ways you can ensure that the impression you make during interviews is a favorable one.

▪ Don't interview on campus. Your on-campus interviewer will probably be a recent graduate of your school who is well acquainted with school policy and standards. Moreover, whether you realize it or not, you will be competing with your fellow classmates. Even attending a selective college won't matter much because all your competitors will have the same credential. By having an off-campus interview you'll reduce the element of competition with students from your school. Off-campus interviewers won't be able to compare achievements readily.

▪ Practice answering the most commonly asked interview questions in front of a mirror or with a friend. Role playing gives you immediate feedback so that you can evaluate and improve your performance.

▪ If you have a choice, pick the last or first interviewing session of the day. Studies reveal that people remember best those events that occur at the end and the beginning of a series. Whatever you do, don't request the session immediately before lunch; the only thing the interviewer will remember about the session will be his hunger pains.

- Read the literature on each company you apply to and come prepared with questions. The last question you'll be asked is, "Do you have any questions of your own?" Don't, however, ask questions that are answered in the company's brochure; you'll look unprepared.

- Don't drink any alcoholic beverages the night before your interview because you want to be as coherent as possible.

- Dress neatly, and be clean and conservative. Don't wear anything tight or low-cut. Don't overlook minor details (like clean eyeglass lenses and neatly manicured nails). An interview is based mostly on first impressions, and studies show that people believe that good-looking men and women also possess other desirable traits (e.g., intelligence, honesty, and compassion). Look your best in order to make a good first impression.

- Don't wear any cologne.

- Bring a couple of copies of your resume to give to the recruiter and to remind yourself of details. You might also want to bring your recommendations and references.

- Find out the interviewer's name so that you can greet him appropriately. He'll be impressed.

- Obtain the phone number of the company so that you can give your interviewer a call in case you are delayed en route to the interview.

- If you have visual aids to document your accomplishments, bring them with you to the interview. People usually have a strong visually-oriented memory.

- Arrive on time.

- Introduce yourself and firmly shake hands with the interviewer. A firm handshake conveys a feeling of warmth, enthusiasm, and confidence. How would you feel if you were handed a limp fish in a handshake?

• Never smoke or glance down at your watch.

• Sit up straight, smile, make eye contact (this doesn't mean stare), be enthusiastic, and act confident.

• Be personable.

• Think about the question before you speak. Many people fall into the trap of volunteering too much information about themselves. Expand on a point only if it will clarify your experiences and skills as they relate to the job. You shouldn't talk for more than 40 percent of the interview. Try to get the interviewer to talk also. Ask questions such as, "What is it like to work here?" and "What types of qualities/traits would be ideal for a successful career with this company?" You should prepare and memorize at least two dozen questions.

• Try to steer the conversation in the direction of your interests and strengths.

• Use proper English. Be careful not to use slang or improper grammar.

• At the end of the session, thank the interviewer for her time. Send a follow-up thank you letter within a twenty-four-hour period. Mention your interviewer's name and the topics she seemed most receptive and eager to talk about during the interview. This will help the interviewer remember you. After all, your recruiter might see up to ten prospectives each day; soon each will become a blur.

SAVING AND MANAGING MONEY

No matter how much money you have and earn, you'll need to know how to save and manage it. Since for most students this is the first time they have ever handled their own finances, problems often arise; after a few false starts however, they learn to make a budget and stick to it, balance a checkbook, and pay their bills on time.

Your first step in managing and saving money is to open a bank account. For convenience, don't keep your money in an out-of-state checking account; start one in a bank near your college. Choose a bank with a twenty-four-hour automatic teller machine, a convenient location, and a reputation for friendly service. (Whenever possible, try to use the automatic teller machine during the day. The lines might be longer, but you will be safer. If you have to use the machine late at night, don't go alone—bring a friend.) I recommend a checking account instead of a savings account because, although the latter earns interest, the former allows you to write and cash checks against your balance, a necessity for paying bills. Each month you will receive your cancelled checks along with a bank statement summarizing the month's transactions and your balance. Hold onto your cancelled checks; they serve as your proof of payment.

There are a number of types of checking accounts from which to choose. Before you pick one, ask questions like: Is there a charge for writing checks? Are there monthly charges? Do you have to keep a minimum balance? if so, how much? What are the penalties for falling under this minimum?

Here are some additional tips for saving and managing money:

• Keep a credit card for only bona fide emergencies. If you don't have enough cash on hand or sufficient funds in your checking account, don't buy the item. You'll be more reluctant to part with money that you have (and can touch) than money you don't have (and can't touch). Furthermore, if you have to walk a mile from a record store to your dorm to get the cash to buy the new album you just saw, you'll think twice before going through all that trouble. It is too tempting and too easy to overspend with a credit card (most people spend 34 percent more than they would have if they didn't own a credit card); you just don't realize that over time, even the smallest purchases, when added up, can put you in serious debt.

• Formulate a weekly budget that you review and revise periodically. List only those items that are necessary; this way you'll think twice before you buy anything frivolous.

• Buy used textbooks. They are usually sold at a substantial discount (about 25 percent off the regular price) and most are in pretty good condition (some look like they've never been opened). Don't, however, buy books that have been extensively highlighted or underlined because you learn more when you mark up your book yourself. Make sure to get to the bookstore before the semester begins because used books go quickly.

• Don't sell your books back to the bookstore; sell them to students. Advertise with posters around campus. Bookstores usually buy back books at a piddling sum and then resell them for much more. By cutting out the middleman, both you and the students you sell your books to will save money. If you are an enterprising student, you can even start a business buying and selling used books for more attractive prices than can be had at the bookstores.

• Bring your school supplies from home. Your college bookstore and the stores around your college will be much more expensive.

• Save your receipts from the bookstore. You won't be able to return new books for courses you've dropped without a receipt. Very often professors don't order enough textbooks and the bookstore must reorder the title. By the time the second shipment arrives, you may be behind in the assignments. Therefore, you should buy all the required books and readings for every class you're thinking of taking. Keep all the receipts; if you decide to drop a class or two, you can return the unnecessary books and get a full refund.

• Also save bank statements, cancelled checks, warranties, guarantees, and contracts. Put them in a special folder so that you can find them easily in case you have to refer to them.

• Whenever possible buy used merchandise. In addition to books, you can easily purchase used refrigerators, desks, and chairs for a reasonable price. During the spring many seniors eager to sell their dormitory furniture and old books will post signs all around campus.

• Don't buy recommended books. Ask your professor to put a few copies on reserve in the college library. Most will comply with this request because they understand the financial straits students are often in. Since there is barely enough time in the semester to read the required material, many students won't even bother with the recommended readings; therefore, if you're ahead in your assignments and want to read the recommended texts, you won't face any wait or hassle in obtaining them at the library.

• Before you write a check, make sure you have enough money in your account to cover it. Not only is it embarrassing to write a bad check; it's also expensive. After writing each check, fill out its accompanying stub so you won't have to wait until your monthly bank statement comes to find out how much money you have in your account.

▪ Don't withdraw a large sum of money at one time from your checking account. No matter how much money you have in your pocket, somehow you'll find a way to spend it all.

▪ Whenever you get a check (e.g., from your job or your parents), immediately deposit it in the bank. If you leave it around, you'll be sure to spend or lose it.

▪ Whether or not you live on campus, stay on the meal plan. It's cheaper than cooking for yourself because the cafeteria works on an all-you-can-eat basis. If you insist on going off the meal plan, use

food coupons, buy in quantity, and share expenses and food with your roommate.

- Don't go on shopping sprees with your friends. You'll be tempted to buy things you don't need.

- Don't bring a car. Insurance, gas, and maintenance costs make having a car extremely expensive for a student on a modest budget. Furthermore, many of your friends and acquaintances will ask you to drive them places; sometimes you'll find it very difficult to refuse. Another problem to consider is parking. Many colleges prohibit first-year students from having a car on campus because parking is so difficult and expensive. It is cheaper and more convenient to use a bicycle, bus, or the campus shuttle service for transportation.

- When you travel by air, your savings will be substantial if you reserve plane tickets far in advance. Around vacation time, your school's bulletin boards will be full of "For Sale" signs for plane tickets students want to sell. You'll probably save a lot if you find a ticket you can use. On the other hand, if you intend to go home by car, you might want to consider sharing the ride with a friend who is willing to help defray some of the costs.

- Keep your phone calls to a minimum. Here are some tips to help you save money on phone bills:

  - Call when the rates are cheaper. After 11 p.m. on weekdays, all day Saturday and before 5 p.m. Sunday are the cheapest times.

  - If your parents foot the bill, don't call them collect. Have a preplanned time when they should call you. You'll look forward to hearing from them. For those times when you can't wait until this agreed-upon calling time, work out a plan whereby you give them one ring, hang up, and then wait for them to call you back.

  - Before you call, make a list of the things you want to say so you don't forget anything.

  - Direct the conversation. If you are paying the bill, you should choose the topics you want to discuss. When you call, don't let a family member make a long digression on the difficulties of constructing a dog house.

• Keep a timer by the phone so you can keep track of how much time you are spending.

• Write letters instead. Carry a notepad and jot down things throughout the day.

Warning: Carefully look at your phone bill before you pay it. Many times phone companies charge you for the phone calls made by the student who now occupies your old dormitory room. Also, if you live with a roommate don't volunteer to put your name on the phone (or any other utility) bill. Otherwise, you might get a bad credit rating if your roommate isn't prompt with payments.

13

Your Major and Career

Many colleges require students to declare their major at the end of the sophomore year or at the start of the junior year. Others require students to choose a tentative major at the end of their second term. Those students who want a degree in engineering, architecture, or another specialized field may have to decide during the first semester of freshman year or risk having to take summer school courses in addition to an extra college semester or so.

Choosing your major is a very important step because it will be a factor in the employment and graduate school admissions process. You will need to make a well informed, thoughtful decision; don't be hasty. Many freshmen quickly choose a major for the security making the decision affords; your parents might also put pressure on you to choose something. As a freshman, however, you should keep a few majors in mind without committing yourself to any one. Explore and leave your options open. You will change your mind often, maybe even daily. Don't envy those students who seem to have their course of study and life already planned; you can be assured that they haven't explored all their study options and avenues as you will have when you finally decide.

STEPS IN DECIDING ON A MAJOR

Here is a step-by-step guideline to help you choose your concentration:

Step 1: Acquaint yourself with the majors offered by your school by skimming through the course catalog. Your college will offer a smorgasbord of standard, unusual, and specialized concentration choices.

Step 2: Keep in mind the type of courses and activities you enjoy while you shop for a program of study. The most important criterion in deciding on a major is your enjoyment of the subject. Not only will you have to spend at least two years of your life studying the subject but you might be required to write a senior thesis, which involves extensive research in the library, laboratory, and/or field for one or two semesters. Furthermore, you will find an added benefit in choosing a subject you enjoy; those who enjoy what they do often excel in it.

Step 3: Investigate the requirements for those subjects that interest you. Note the number of theses, papers, upper-level courses, labs, seminars, or volunteer work needed for the degree. Project the schedules you will have to follow for each field. For instance, if you decide to major in psychology, will you be overloaded with requirements during your senior year—senior thesis, advanced labs and seminars?

Step 4: Sample courses from as many different disciplines as possible. Only by taking courses in different subjects will you discover those in which you excel and like. You might even want to design your own unusual course of independent study with faculty sponsorship.

Step 5: Join a few extracurricular activities. Often an extracurricular involvement sparks an idea for or an interest in a certain discipline. For instance, writing for the school's daily newspaper might lead to a concentration (and maybe even a career) in journalism. An internship or summer or term-time job can also broaden your base of choices.

Step 6: Talk to upperclassmen who are majoring in the fields you are considering. They will be able to give you inside information on the professors, requirements, electives, and alternatives. They can also tell you which courses in your school tend to be easy or hard. Keep in mind your strengths and weaknesses; Aquatic Basketweaving 101 might be easy for some, but you may not be able to coordinate your breathing with your weaving. Ask older students such questions as:

- How difficult are the requirements?
- How is performance evaluated in the majority of the courses? For example, English courses tend to require many term papers and chemistry courses have numerous labs.
- What aspects of the discipline tend to be stressed the most?
- Which courses and professors do you recommend?
- How strong is the department?
- Is the department large and impersonal?
- How much more difficult is the Bachelor of Science degree compared to the Bachelor of Arts degree?
- What types of jobs can recent graduates in that subject obtain?

Step 7: Talk to professors and concentration advisors. The concentration advisors for the various departments are professors specially trained to assist students in choosing a program of study. You will meet most of these concentration advisors at their respective departmental open houses. Some of these advisors will be terrific salesmen; they may have to push their departments because they are underenrolled or not very good. You shouldn't make any type of decision solely on the basis of a few talks with your advisor. Get other opinions.

Step 8: Take some upper-level courses in the major you're thinking of choosing. Since introductory courses cover a wide array of topics, most students will find some aspects of the course enjoyable. Advanced courses, however, focus on very specific subtopics, some which you will find boring. Your college might only offer one or two advanced level courses on your favorite topic(s).

Step 9: Keep in mind your career goals as you choose a major. If you plan to enter the job market upon graduation, your major and peripheral courses of study will probably be especially important. Those students who intend to apply to medical, law, or business school, however, may concentrate in anything. (For further information on pre-professional courses of study such as law, medicine, and business, see the following sections in this chapter.)

Many employers prefer to hire graduates with some type of previous experience; your major may help you land certain types of jobs. An economics major trying for a financial analyst position will have a slight edge over an art history major applying for the same job. If the art history major, however, has a background in a business-related field (e.g., a few upper-level courses in economics or an internship or summer job in an investment banking firm), she will no longer be at a disadvantage.

After graduation, students often find themselves in training programs or positions for which they had no previous training or exposure. For many companies, enthusiasm and the ability to think well and learn fast are still the traits most admired in prospective employees.

Concentration advisors, career placement counselors, alumni in your prospective careers, and recent graduates will be able to advise you on the type of employment opportunities available to someone with your abilities and interests.

Step 10: If you don't find a standard concentration that interests you, consider designing your own interdisciplinary concentration (e.g., Folklore or Law, Health, and Society) with a cohesive theme. Since you will need faculty sponsorship and academic committee approval in order to file your independent concentration, you should start planning early.

Step 11: Don't let your parents pressure you into choosing a certain major. Some students practically have their parents choose their major for them. Unfortunately for these students, their parents can't also complete the tests, papers, labs, projects, research, quizzes, and thesis required for the degree. Listen to and consider their advice (just as you would your advisors or dean), but decide for yourself what you want to study. Too often students who declare a certain major in order to please their parents realize later that they either hate the subject or have no aptitude for it. Ultimately, they have to pick another major.

Step 12: Explore the academic reputations of each department. Is your school's mathematics department and program notoriously weak or understaffed? Is the computer science department especially innovative or the political science department nationally acclaimed? Obviously, if you major in a well-known and respected department with award-winning faculty, you benefit.

CHANGING YOUR MAJOR

Many students declare a certain major after taking only a few introductory courses in the subject. When, however, these same students begin to delve further into their chosen field, they don't enjoy it as much, if at all. If you aren't happy with your major, you should change it even if it means a setback of a year or two. Don't stick it out just to say you finished it; you will only make yourself unhappy. You will also find it harder to get good grades in your major once you've lost interest in it. You will be inclined to miss classes, party when you really should study, forget academic deadlines, and remain quiet during classroom discussions if your studies hold no interest and bring no sense of satisfaction.

After you decide what department you want to switch to, you need to assess your situation. How many courses have you already taken in your proposed concentration? If the answer is not many, will you have to stretch college out for another year or can you make up the credits during summer school? Can you formulate an independent concentration with some of the courses you've already taken? Will you have time to write a thesis if you so choose?

You will need to discuss these concerns with a concentration advisor or dean. Although switching majors entails tons of extra work, administrative as well as academic, you will undoubtedly find the change beneficial.

CHOOSING A CAREER

Like many of your classmates, you probably don't have the slightest inkling about your future career goals. This is fine. You should, however, start investigating your career possibilities because some, such as medicine and engineering, require extensive undergraduate preparation.

Since your career choice should be based on your abilities, interests, and background, your chosen program of study will probably be the best indicator of the type of career you'd enjoy and succeed in. If you already know what you will probably major in,

find out what types of jobs are available in light of your choice of study. For instance, if you like math and economics you might enjoy investment banking or financial consulting. Visit your college career center as soon as possible. It will have descriptions of interesting jobs you didn't even know existed and can give you a test to help you determine what type of career would suit you best.

Before you choose a career direction, look into the type of preparation the career requires. If you intend to enter a certain job market immediately after graduation, you might want to think about how marketable your major will make you. In some fields, employers prefer students who major in certain subjects; for instance, an accounting firm won't want a Russian literature major. If, however, you are a Russian lit major who took a number of upper-level accounting courses, you might even the odds.

Employers in some fields, however, don't show any preference for one major over another. An international relations major and an economics major will both be in the running for a position in journalism. After graduation, many liberal arts majors find themselves in fields they've never dreamed about.

A growing number of students each year decide to delay entry into the job market for a few years. If you are considering graduate, medical, law, or business school, the following sections may be helpful.

GRADUATE SCHOOL

Some seniors delay employment for a number of years in order to attend graduate school and earn a master's or a Ph.D. The number of graduates who want to teach or do research has decreased in the last decade and is expected to continue dropping. One reason is that professors don't make a lot of money, and thus some departments, such as chemistry and physics, must heavily recruit overseas for students.

Although you don't necessarily have to major in the subject you wish to pursue at the graduate level, you should take some courses in the field. Otherwise, neither you nor the graduate school admissions committee will know whether you are proficient in the subject or not. Some graduate schools welcome a class with a diversity of academic backgrounds. Nonetheless, many of the students who apply to graduate school for a given subject not only major in that subject but also write a thesis and do extensive outside research in it. Whether you pursue a master's degree or a doctor of philosophy degree, you will be required to write some sort of dissertation or thesis in your chosen field. You might want to write an undergraduate thesis because it not only allows you to graduate with honors (in some schools) but also shows graduate school admissions officers that you have the initiative to undertake research on your own. Some undergraduate students have even made discoveries of major importance while doing their thesis (two undergrads discovered the echolocation system of bats while doing research for their thesis).

In order to make yourself even more attractive to graduate school admissions committees, you should consider getting some outside experience in your field of inquiry. Mike, a prospective organic chemistry major, wanted a summer research internship in organic chemistry. He went to a few of his professors and asked them if they needed a summer researcher. One of his professors not only wanted a summer researcher but a term-time one as well. Hands-on experience ultimately helped Mike decide to pursue a major and career in organic chemistry.

MEDICAL SCHOOL

If you contemplate a career in one of the medical fields, you will need to start preparing early, preferably in your freshman or sophomore year. You will have to meet pre-medical requirements before you apply to medical, dental, or veterinary schools. Most schools require a year of biology with lab, inorganic chemistry with lab, physics with lab, organic chemistry with lab, possibly calculus, and an advanced biology course. These requirements (especially organic chemistry) serve as weeders; they are difficult courses designed to discourage all but the truly dedicated. Since they can't be laughed off as Mickey Mouse courses (prepare to sweat for five hours in organic chemistry lab alone), it is best to start your pre-med program in your freshman year. Those who decide to go into medicine in their junior or senior year often have to finish some of the requirements during the summer and after graduation.

Although the number of medical school applications has steadily declined in the last ten years, the competition is still quite cutthroat. Many American medical schools require students to maintain a B average. This often causes pre-med syndrome; students become so competitive that they won't even lend a fellow classmate notes. There have been reports of pre-meds sabotaging their classmates' notebooks and other academic evildoings. As a result, you will notice that only a fraction of those who were in your freshman biology class will stay pre-med long enough to apply to medical school.

As long as you successfully complete all the pre-med courses, medical school admissions committees don't care what major you select. Every year many liberal arts majors enter medical schools. Most pre-meds, however, major in biology, neural science, or some other related science, since many of the requirements for medical school and these majors often coincide. I recommend that you not major in a science. Because most of your pre-med classmates will be majoring in these subjects, the competition will be extremely keen. Furthermore, you will find that those students who major in the sciences (especially the hard sciences) have lower averages than those who major in the liberal arts.

If you are thinking about a career as a health professional, you need to talk to your school's pre-med advisor as soon as possible. Your pre-med advisor will be able to tell you what you should be doing to prepare for medical school. In addition to helping you outline your pre-med program, she will provide you with your school's medical school admission statistics.

Every year the top medical schools in the country review many applicants with very near perfect GPAs and MCAT scores. How do they choose among these qualified students? They make a subjective decision based on the applicant's teacher recommendations, extracurricular activities, summer and term-time job experiences, honors, awards, and other activities and achievements.

The recommendations you ultimately send off with your application will be from professors who taught you recently (i.e., junior year). If, however, you seem to be doing outstanding work in one of your freshman or sophomore courses (especially one that fulfills a pre-med requirement), ask the instructor to write you a recommendation and place it in your permanent academic file. You might want this recommendation to accompany your application later on. So cultivate good relationships with a few of your professors. Otherwise, your recommendations won't be much more than a reiteration of your test scores. Your pre-med advisor will also write one of your medical school recommendations, so whenever you meet with him, formally or otherwise, try to make a good impression.

To further strengthen your future medical school application, you should try to get involved in some activities during your freshman and sophomore years. Don't, however, become active in too many organizations and groups (especially during the hectic freshman year), because you won't be able to dedicate enough time to them all. Since your goal will be to achieve a leadership position in one or two of your extracurricular pursuits, you will need to concentrate your energies.

During the summer, you will also need to do something else

besides laze around under the sun. Work in a lab or volunteer in a hospital over the summer and during your January break. Since most of your pre-medical courses probably won't prepare you for any of the medical field's practical aspects (except maybe the all-night study and rounds session), most med schools will ask you about your health care experience (for example, have you worked or volunteered in a hospital, clinic, or doctor's office?) Your clinical experience might help you decide if medicine is really what you want.

Before you start your pre-med program, think carefully about your reasons for becoming a doctor. Are you motivated by the money and prestige associated with the medical profession or by a sincere desire to help others? Are your parents pressuring you to become a doctor? Carefully examine your motives now. You don't want to realize in your junior year, after finishing all your pre-med requirements and lowering your average, that you hate the practical aspects of medicine. Unfortunately, some people actually manage to delude themselves even through the six grueling years of medical school and internship.

LAW SCHOOL

Since many students are opting for the law profession, the competition to get into law school has become unbelievable. Because the best jobs tend to go to graduates of the prestigious law schools (Harvard, Yale, Stanford, Colombia, the University of Chicago, New York University, and the University of Pennsylvania), the percentage of applicants accepted to these schools has dwindled.

Law schools, unlike medical schools, don't have any special requirements. Although English, history, and political science are very popular with pre-law students, feel free to take and major in whatever you want. You must, however, strive to get good grades in whatever you choose; a good average and LSAT (Law School Admission Test) score are the major factors in law school admissions. The Law Schools Admissions Service (LSAS), the nationwide clearing center for the LSAT and law school application information, formulates an index for each law school applicant based on LSAT score and G.P.A. Law schools, however, may also take into consideration such information as the applicant's extracurricular activities, recommendations, work experience, and honors and awards. The best application is one that shows a prolonged concentration in one field or study. For instance, the student who has extracurricular activities, work experience, and honors, all in the field of Slavic studies, will have a stronger application than someone who has activities, work, and honors in several disciplines. Indeed, the most prestigious law schools, which receive applications from many students with perfect or very near-perfect LSATs and G.P.A.s, may have no other recourse but to reject or accept applications solely on the basis of the subjective information.

If you decide to pursue a career in law, you'll need to keep your grades up, join a couple of extracurricular activities with the explicit purpose of gaining a leadership position by your junior or senior year, cultivate a good student/professor rapport to be reasonably assured of highly personalized recommendations, and gain summer work experience, preferably involving many responsibilities. Sometime during your freshman year, visit your pre-law advisor and ask for the law school admissions statistics for your school. This will give you a good idea of the grades you'll need for each law school.

Some students don't apply to law school until many years after they graduate from college. Many of these older applicants have acquired very impressive credentials during these years. For instance, you might have spent your time receiving a Ph.D. in English and then working as a lecturer in a prestigious university. If you intend to apply to law schools later, plan to accomplish some worthwhile goals during the interim. Law schools are bound to ask you what you have done, what you have learned, and what you have accomplished.

BUSINESS SCHOOL

Business schools, like medical and law schools, don't require students to major in any specific subject, but a couple of courses in accounting, economics, and business can prove helpful. However, most business schools require applicants for the Masters in Business Administration (M.B.A.) to have practical business experience.

Since business schools insist on extensive job experience, employer recommendations count heavily in the admissions process. Unfortunately, most students aren't able to acquire the needed business experience before they graduate from college. As a result, many take full-time employment in a bank, stock brokerage, or insurance company for a couple of years before applying to business schools. Every year, however, a few applicants enter right from college. These exceptional cases have extensive relevant summer and term-time employment during their undergraduate years. If you feel you have sufficient experience, you might want to apply to schools in your senior year. You will either be rejected, accepted, or accepted conditionally (provided you work for two years in the business world beforehand).

Aside from doing well in your courses, you should start getting involved in the business aspects of some campus organizations (i.e., school newspaper and student shops and associations). You can become the business manager or accounts manager of a campus publication. A few truly enterprising students even start their own business; there are college students who have thriving printing, computer software, and publishing businesses. You can, too!

MAJOR AND CAREER PLANNING CALENDAR
FOR YOUR FRESHMAN AND SOPHOMORE YEARS

Freshman Year

Summer:

• If you don't know how to type or use a computer, take a course at your local high school. No matter what subjects you study, these skills will be necessary.

• Preregister for your courses on time. Otherwise, you will be closed out of the more desirable limited-enrollment courses.

• If you intend to take any placement tests in September, brush up now.

• Prepare yourself, mentally and emotionally, for your transition from high school to college. Get advice and information from an older sibling or a friend who currently attends your new college.

September–November:

- Enjoy orientation. Make friends with residential counselors, dormmates, and upperclassmen.

- Take placement tests.

- Visit the career placement office early to get the best pick of on-campus employment.

- Investigate your school's extracurricular opportunities. Go to your school's activities fair and sign up for those activities that interest you. Ultimately, you should choose only one or two of them.

- Shop around for courses. Ask upperclassmen for their opinions concerning courses. Read course and teacher evaluations. Try to choose your program from a wide array of subjects. If, however, you want to be an engineer, architect, doctor, or veterinarian, start preparing now.

- Write down all your registration deadlines (i.e., grade changing and add-drop) on your calendar.

- Stay at least a week ahead in all your school work. Many students get sick with a flu or virus the first year because they are under much pressure, partying and socializing too much, or living in a crowded dormitory where germs spread easily.

- Get a student tutor for those courses in which you need help. You will find the rates to be either free or very, very reasonable because student tutoring programs are often subsidized by the college.

- Get to know your professors and deans.

- If you are having roommate difficulties, talk to your residential counselor before the problems start to affect your schoolwork.

December:

- Start studying early for your finals. You might want to form study groups for those subjects that lend themselves to roundtable discussions.

- Preregister for next semester's classes.

• Start thinking about summer employment. Make an appointment with a career placement counselor who will be able to assist you in finding a job and perfecting a resume.

• Enjoy your holidays.

February–April:

• Once again, shop carefully for your courses. Continue to take courses under those professors with whom you've done well; good impressions are hard to erase.

• Further involve yourself in your extracurricular activities.

• Ask your professor for job recommendations or referrals.

• If you become itchy with transferitis, send for the appropriate college catalogs and applications.

• You might want to apply to be a residential counselor.

• Actively seek out summer employment. Make phone calls, send out resumes, and go on interviews. Continue to check your career placement office for new summer job listings.

May:

• Cultivate good professor/student relationships.

• Ask your professors to write recommendations for your permanent file.

• Although spring is in full bloom, continue to attend classes to the very last day.

• Study hard for finals. Many freshmen goof off because they believe that their first year's grades won't matter much, if at all. Wrong! This year's grades will count for graduate schools, employment, scholarships, fellowships, and honor societies.

• Ask your friends and upperclassmen for their old class notes and tests before they throw them away. Save your notes so that you can swap.

• Prepare yourself to work hard in your summer job so that your employer will write you a good recommendation.

• Make it a goal to learn one new skill or acquire a new interest this summer.

Sophomore Year

September–November:

• Keep in touch with your professors from last year. You might need their help in the future.

• Make a tentative plan outlining your goals for the next three years.

• Since this is the time when the notorious sophomore slump hits, make a vow to work extra hard in your classes.

• Choose your courses carefully. This is the time to think about narrowing your academic focus; you'll have to declare a major at the end of this year.

• Since your courses this semester will be more advanced and smaller in size, actively participate in class discussions.

• Concentrate on attaining a high position in your extracurricular activities.

• Attend some departmental open houses and introduce yourself to the faculty members.

• If you are interested in designing an independent concentration, start looking for faculty sponsors now.

December:

• Continue to cultivate good professor/student relationships. Talk to your instructors after class, participate in classroom discussions, and make appointments to discuss your academic concerns during office hours.

• Study superhard for your final exams because your final exam grades often determine your final course grades. (Some final exams are worth 75 percent of your final grade.)

• Visit the career planning office, and send out resumes for summer jobs.

• Have a wonderful vacation.

February–April:

• Make sure you have some type of employment or activity planned for the summer. You might want to enroll in a work camp or overseas summer study program.

• If you intend to study abroad or participate in an internship during your junior year, talk to your advisor about finding a suitable program.

• Get applications for those scholarships and awards for which you qualify.

May:

• Start studying for your finals in advance. Finish researching and writing your final term papers. Don't wait until the very last minute when you will also have to cram for finals.

• Preregister for next year's courses. Make sure to evenly space out the more difficult requirements.

- Declare your concentration.

- Talk to career advisors, upperclassmen, and professors about graduate studies. Write for graduate school catalogs and applications.

- Have a fun, productive summer.

14

Alternative Study Opportunities

Students who want to pursue a course of study not offered by the university have the option, with committee approval and faculty sponsorship, of devising their own course and/or concentration. Students, however, should be aware that proposals for independent studies and concentration require careful planning and enormous amounts of work. Often students find themselves revising their proposals repeatedly before eventually receiving committee approval. Furthermore, students who want to do an independent concentration are required to do a special project, usually a thesis. If you do decide to do an independent study or concentration you will find the experience quite pleasurable and educational, as well as unforgettable. In this chapter we will look at other study opportunities such as internships, summer school courses, foreign study, and so on.

INTERNSHIPS

Since most college courses are confined to the realm of the academic, internships give students a unique opportunity to acquire hands-on job experience before graduation. Students can be placed in practically any type of organization imaginable (i.e., public relations, government, education, scientific research, and health care). Most students choose to intern in a field in which they intend to ultimately work; indeed, many students take employment with these very organizations and companies after graduation. Your college's career placement office or resource center will have a list of various types of available internships (i.e., volunteer/paid, full-time/part-time and credit/non-credit). If you want to receive credit for your work, you will probably be required to write a term paper examining a major issue you encountered while doing your internship. Therefore, be sure to check out thoroughly the types of duties you will perform; the more responsibility and creativity involved, the better. You don't want to take a semester to a year off to just spread peat moss around an organic farm in Wyoming. Moreover, you aren't only confined to the standard internships listed. You can design your own internship by approaching an organization on your own. In order to get college credit for an internship of your own design, you will probably need a faculty sponsor.

SUMMER SCHOOL

In addition to the regular term-time session, virtually every school in the country offers a summer session. Luckily, summer school doesn't quite have the same reputation for college students that it does for high school and grammar school students. Many of your classmates consider it much more enjoyable than summer employment. You may, however, decide to attend summer school for reasons besides just avoiding work. Students flock to classes during the summer for a number of reasons:

• Since the course offerings at various schools differ, a student might find the "perfect" course at another college.

• For students on academic probation, summer school is an opportunity to catch up on graduation credits.

• With enough summer school credits, some students become eligible to graduate a semester early.

• Courses in organic and inorganic chemistry and foreign languages are very time-consuming in terms of labs, classes, and sections. Fitting these courses into a regular schedule can be difficult.

▪ During the summer, students can repeat classes they failed or almost failed.

▪ Since students take only one or two classes during the summer, as opposed to four or five during a semester, they can devote more time to each subject. As a result, students can boost their G.P.A.s.

▪ Students don't have to transfer their summer school grades if they so choose.

For all these reasons, summer studies can seem most desirable. You should know, however, that there are some hidden disadvantages:

▪ Most classes aren't air-conditioned. This can become a major concern as you steam a chemical concoction in 90° weather for an organic chemistry experiment.

▪ For the most part, the campuses are deserted during the summer.

▪ Your school for one reason (money) or another (money) may not grant you credit for studies taken at another school. Thus, if you want credit your only choice may be to take your summer school classes at your school. If your school happens to be far away from home, however, you will need to pay for room and board in addition to tuition.

▪ You may end up suffering from academic burnout.

▪ Since summer school sessions last only a couple of months at the most, you must study at a hectic pace. As a result, most students don't have enough free time for a full-time job and can't save money for the following semester.

▪ Many of the best professors refuse to teach summer sessions. They reserve their summers for research.

▪ If you study at a school other than your regular school, you will be at a disadvantage because you won't know your professors or your way around.

▪ Suppose you take two courses at your local university and do well in one course and poorly in the other. You won't be able to hide the bad grade if you want credit for the good grade, because both will appear on your summer school transcript.

If you eventually decide to take a couple of summer school courses at another school, make sure the credits are transferable. My last piece of advice is to apply for the summer sessions early. Otherwise, you may be left holding the proverbial bag.

TRANSFERITIS

If your school's academic program doesn't fulfill your needs, you might want to consider transferring. Transferitis seems to plague every freshman and sophomore at one time or another. Although it can hit anytime, it usually bothers students the most during the beginning of their first semester and around finals time. For the majority of students, however, bouts of transferitis are short-lived and disappear quickly with the help of a few good friends.

A small percentage of students at every school, however, suffers from chronic transferitis. If this happens to you, examine your reasons for wanting to transfer. Virtually every transfer application asks why; your chances of acceptance will be greater if you can cite some compelling academic reason(s) for your request. Occasionally, the trouble lies within yourself, not your academic surroundings. Although a few students have such an awesome academic reputation or some other quality that the transfer school will accept him or her regardless of everything else, most college transfer admissions committees automatically reject applicants who give ridiculous and/ or insincere reasons for seeking a transfer. Some situations in which a transfer can prove helpful are these:

- The school you currently attend is either very weak in or doesn't offer the specific program of study you wish to pursue.
- You wish to go to a more prestigious university.
- Financial assistance from your current school has proved to be insufficient.
- You have specific and compelling social reasons (i.e., you prefer a coed college or you want to join your spouse at his or her university).

Even if you have a good reason for wanting to transfer, you should think carefully before you do anything; there are many problems inherent in transferring. For example, you will receive last pick of courses and on-campus housing. Not all of your courses will be transferred, and you may need to stay in school an extra semester or so to make up the lost credits. Since it takes about a semester to adjust fully to your new campus, your grades may suffer. In addition, you will have to make all types of social adjustments once again.

If, however, you decide to transfer, you will find the admissions process very similar to the one you went through as a high school senior. Your college transcript, however, will be more important than your high school record. Since many of the most prestigious universities have as many as twenty applicants for each place, recommendations, awards, honors, and extracurricular activities will be taken into consideration in addition to your reasons for wanting a transfer. Talk to friends, students, and professors from those schools you are considering and find out the unique and outstanding qualities of each school. Send for college brochures and applications and visit the various colleges.

FOREIGN STUDY

What better way to enhance your present course of study than with a semester or two of foreign study? Most students who study abroad do so during their junior year. This is the best time because you have already declared your major and know how an overseas program would strengthen your studies. Juniors also don't have the added problems of preparing for graduate school exams, writing applications, or interviewing for post-graduation employment. Finally, by their junior year most students have acquired a moderate degree of proficiency in a foreign language, a requirement of most programs in non-English-speaking countries.

In order to decide from among the many foreign study programs available, you will need to do some preliminary research. Your first step is to go to your school's Office of International Programs and speak to the dean in charge, who will be able to direct you to a list of foreign study programs sponsored by your school and other American institutions. Read each of the brochures carefully, with an eye for selectivity and quality. Disregard programs that aren't approved by your school and for which you won't receive graduation credit; you probably don't want to graduate a semester or two late. As you read through each brochure and talk to your dean, answer these questions:

- What organization is sponsoring the program?
- How competitive is its admission process?
- How are the students chosen? Are all ages accepted? If so, is the program truly selective?
- What is the academic reputation of the program? of the host university?
- How qualified is the faculty?
- What type of living accommodations can you expect? Keep in mind that the standards for adequate housing vary drastically throughout the world.
- Will you go to classes with natives or will you be limited to those classes reserved for American students?
- How much does the program cost? Is financial aid available?

Before you pick a program, talk to upperclassmen who have already participated in it. Ask them some of the questions listed above and have them describe their experience. You might also want to find out which programs the deans and professors of your school recommend. They often know the academic reputation and worth of foreign professors and institutions.

Obviously, some concentrations, such as engineering and computer science, don't lend themselves readily to international studies. However, even if you won't be able to directly apply it to your major, an overseas study program can give you a new perspective on a different culture. You should therefore look into the possibility of participating in an overseas summer program. Those students who aren't fluent in a second language but who want to be might also want to explore some type of international summer language program. You will undoubtedly benefit from your overseas experience, provided you thoroughly research your opportunities and plan ahead.

Index